Wonderful Word Puzzle

MINI-BOOKS

20 REPRODUCIBLE MINI-BOOKS PACKED WITH HIGH-INTEREST ACTIVITIES THAT SHARPEN SKILLS IN VOCABULARY, SPELLING, GRAMMAR, AND MORE!

by Jan Meyer

SCHOLASTIC
PROFESSIONAL BOOKS

New York • Toronto • London • Auckland • Sydney • Mexico City
New Delhi • Hong Kong • Buenos Aires

For Jeffrey, Julia, David,
Lyndsey and Jamie

Cover design by **Gerard Fuchs**
Cover and interior artwork by **Mike Moran**
Interior design by **Holly Grundon**
Literacy consultant **Katherine Schulten**

ISBN: 0-439-37666-1

Printed in the U.S.A.

2 3 4 5 6 7 8 9 10 40 09 08 07 06 05 04 03

Contents

About This Book 4
How to Make the Mini-Books 4
Making the Most of Each Mini-Book . . 5

MINI-BOOKS

Words Within Words
There's a Bird in That Word 11
Wordy Wigglers 13
The Case of the Missing Words . . 15

Homonyms & Multiple Meanings
Mussels With Muscles 17

Prefixes & Suffixes
That's Amazing 19

Rhyming Words
Rhyme Finds 21

Anagrams & Scramblers
Field Trip Scramble 23
Magic Hat Trick 25
Chef Alfonso's Word Recipe 27

Idioms & Similes
Eating Your Words 29

Compound Words
Compound Roundup 31
Barefoot Football 33

Syllables
The Syllable Shuffler 35

Missing Letters
One for All 37
Clueless Crosswords 39

Secret Codes
Crack the Code 41

Antonyms & Synonyms
Zigs & Zags 43
Synonym Search 45

Making Words
Shrink 'Ems 47
Be a Word Wizard 49

ANSWERS 51

About This Book

Welcome to *Word-Puzzle Mini-Books*! This fun classroom supplement is filled with engaging puzzles and activities that:

- ★ cover the language arts topics you teach: spelling, vocabulary, and grammar
- ★ build practice with antonyms, synonyms, homonyms, syllables, prefixes and suffixes
- ★ promote an active involvement and interest in language arts
- ★ stimulate an enjoyment of words—their formation, spelling patterns, sounds and meanings
- ★ demonstrate a variety of ways to have fun "playing" with words
- ★ show students, as well, how words "magically" change, as letters are added, removed, replaced or rearranged

Note:

If a puzzle seems too challenging, work through it as a group.

How to Make the Mini-Books

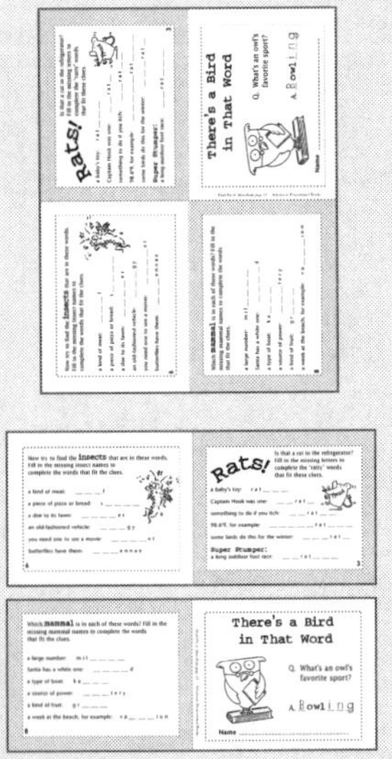

1. Carefully remove the mini-book to be copied, tearing along the perforated line, and make a double-sided copy of the page (one per student).
2. Have students cut apart the pages along the dotted line and then fold the pages along the solid line.
3. Help students assemble the pages in order.
4. Staple the books together along the folded edge.

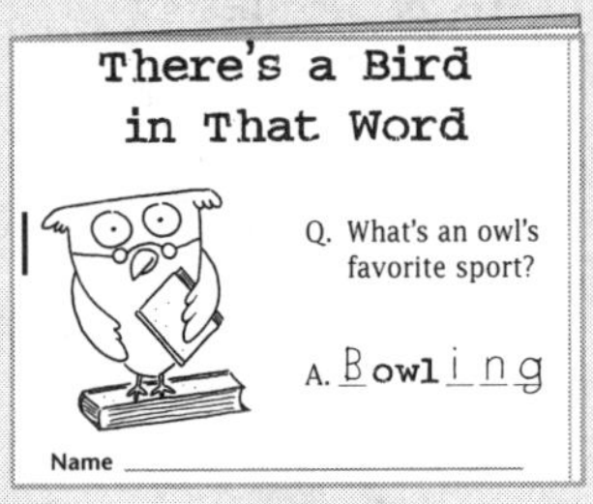

Making the Most of Each Mini-Book

In most of the mini-books, the puzzles are arranged in order of difficulty. This allows students to gain confidence before the challenge increases. Some mini-books include high-challenge bonus puzzles that give students an added sense of achievement when solved. Here's a look at each mini-book:

Words Within Words

THERE'S A BIRD IN THAT WORD!

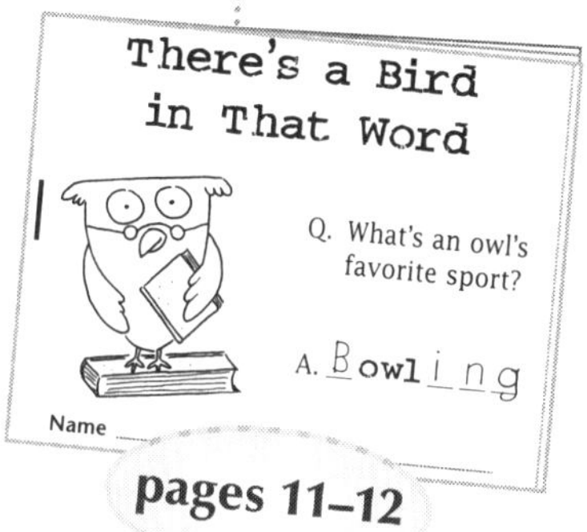

pages 11–12

Students are surprised and amused when they discover that the word "owl" is in "bowling," the word "quit" is in "mosquito," or the word "ogre" is in "progress." Finding words within words is an entertaining way to turn students on to the wonder of language.

This mini-book is filled with birds, insects, rodents, sea creatures and mammals—names of these animals are hiding in different words! Aided by a clue, students fill in missing letters to complete each puzzle word.

As a follow-up activity, make a list of more words in which the words "ant" and "rat" can be found. Words not used in these puzzles include:

ant		rat	
fantasy	grant	ratio	perspiration
cantaloupe	slanted	rather	celebrate
giant	Atlantic	crater	democratic
antelope	Antarctica	grateful	frustrate
anteater	meant	illustration	evaporate
enchanted	frantic	separate	accurate
instant	romantic	considerate	concentrate
distant	pantry	cooperate	decorate
fantastic	anticipate	vibrate	operation
plant	panther	immigration	karate

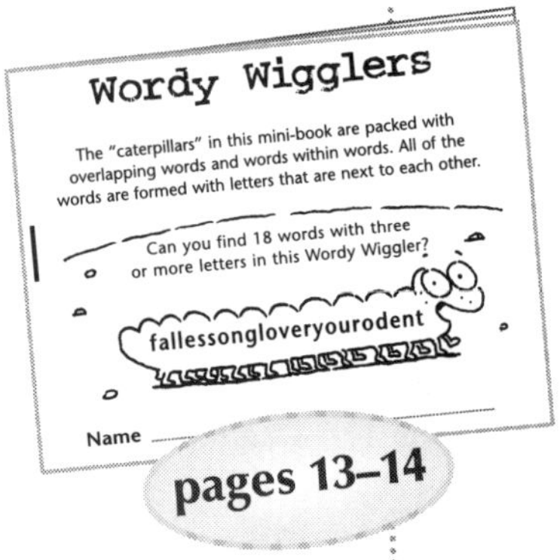

WORDY WIGGLERS

In these puzzles, students find the many overlapping words that are crowded together. To get kids started, the answers to the Wordy Wiggler on the cover page are given.

Encourage students to create their own Wordy Wigglers. They can do this as a class, in groups or on their own. They simply start with a word such as "smile" and then add a word starting with the word's final two letters ("learn" or "letter," for example). Students should try to include words in which there are other words like "butter," "carpet" and "shipment."

THE CASE OF THE MISSING WORDS

Here, students find the words that are missing inside a series of words. Before starting these puzzles, remind students that the pronunciation of a word may change when it is inserted into a word. For example, the pronunciation of the letters in the word "ache" would change if "ache" were inserted to complete the word "mustache."

Homonyms & Multiple Meanings

MUSSELS WITH MUSCLES

Your students will roar when they figure out that a "grizzly that's lost its fur" is a "bare bear." Here, students have fun as they try to answer these homonym puzzles, guess which multiple meaning words fit given double definitions, and illustrate two meanings for a word such as "bat," "fence" or "fly."

Prefixes & Suffixes

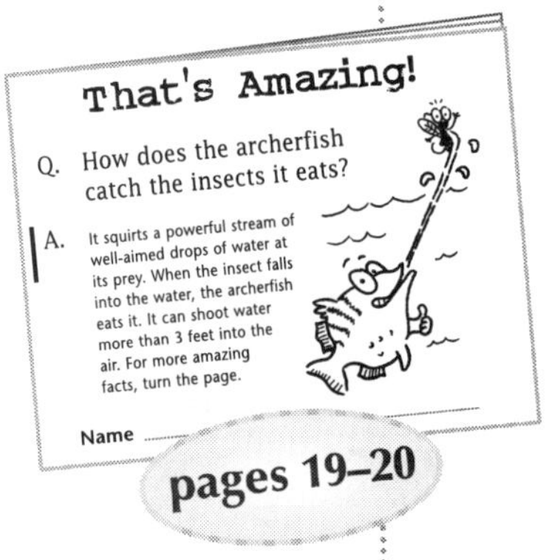

THAT'S AMAZING

This mini-book provides practice with thirty-five different prefixes and suffixes. Motivated to find the amazing answers to questions about animals, students must add a suffix or prefix to change each underlined word to a new word that fits a provided clue.

Rhyming Words

RHYME FINDS

These are word search puzzles with a twist. Rather than looking for words in a word list, students look for unidentified words that rhyme with a given word.

Each grid includes rhyming words with endings that are spelled differently and several words whose endings are spelled the same, but don't rhyme. The last page of this mini-book invites students to create their own rhymes. Caution students to look for rhyming words within rhyming words. For example, inside the word "sphere" is the rhyming word "here" (puzzle page 4).

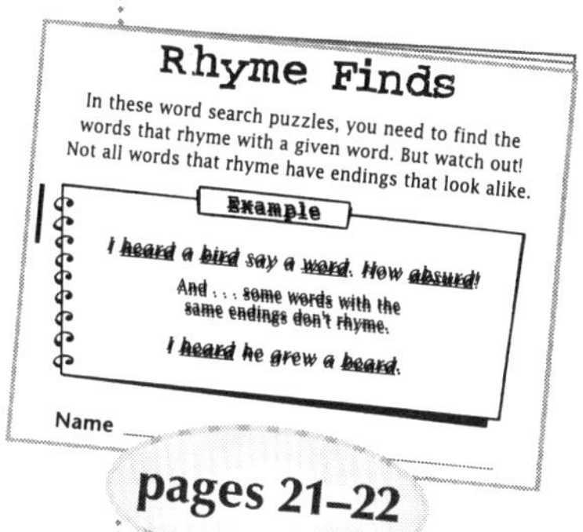

pages 21–22

Anagrams & Scramblers

FIELD TRIP SCRAMBLE

In this mini-book, students set off on seven field trip adventures! On each theme-oriented trip, they unscramble five words and then use letters in their puzzle answers to unscramble a sixth word.

pages 23–24

MAGIC HAT TRICK

In these anagram puzzles, classroom magicians must use all the letters in a five-letter word to make two new words—a two-letter word and a three-letter word. Before they start, tell students that, from many of the five-letter words, more than one anagram can be made. They will find out, as well, that sometimes a two-letter word can be made, but the remaining letters do not form a word.

pages 25–26

CHEF ALFONSO'S WORD RECIPE

In these puzzles, students combine the letters of a four-letter word and a given additional letter to create a five-letter word. Each puzzle page includes a "double the fun" challenge.

pages 27–28

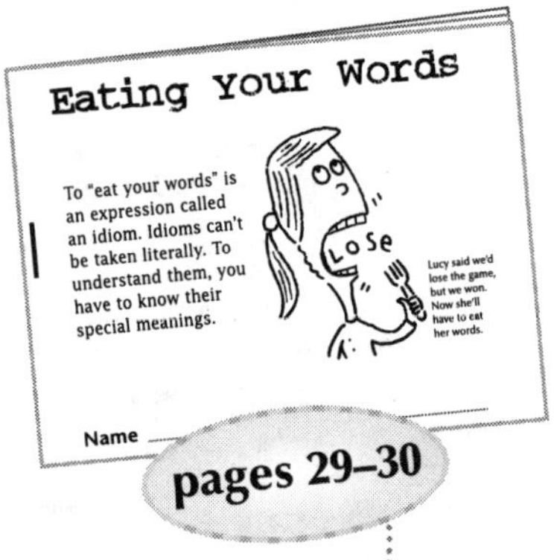

Idioms & Similes

EATING YOUR WORDS

Idioms and similes make our language quirky and colorful! In this mini-book, students complete commonly used idioms and similes with the names of animals, foods and parts of the body. On page 7, children can write their own similes. Because idioms rarely mean what they literally say, students have a chance, on page 8, to illustrate the literal meaning of an idiom of their choice! The primary purpose of this mini-book is to encourage students to have fun with expressive language. Therefore, if they are not familiar with some of the idioms, they should just fill in their best and most creative guesses.

Compound Words

COMPOUND ROUNDUP

These puzzles are similar in format to word search puzzles. Hidden in each of the seven puzzle grids are twenty compound words. Students must find them by joining words in boxes that connect vertically, horizontally or diagonally.

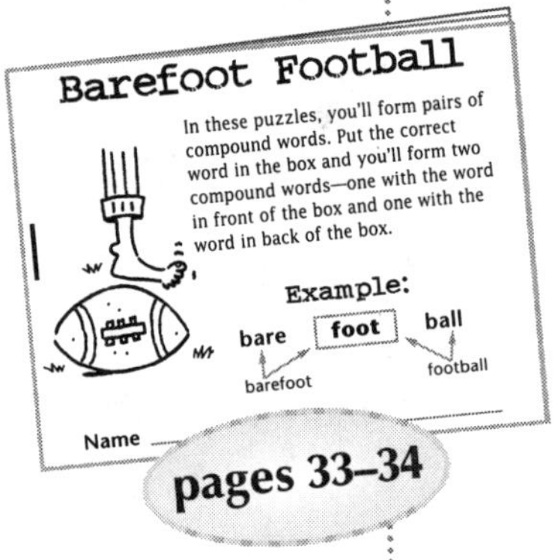

BAREFOOT FOOTBALL

The challenge increases! In these puzzles, students form a series of pairs of compound words. To do this, they supply a missing word between two words that then forms two compound words—one with the word on the left and one with the word on the right.

Example: waste ________ ball

The missing word is "basket," forming the two compound words "wastebasket" and "basketball."

Syllables

THE SYLLABLE SHUFFLER

In these puzzles, students put the correct syllables back together to form three-syllable words. This mini-book is a good introduction to syllable division. In addition, it builds spelling and word formation skills.

Missing Letters

ONE FOR ALL

In this mini-book, students find the one letter that completes all four words in each puzzle row. The missing letter may be an initial consonant, a final consonant, a consonant in the middle of the word, or a part of a consonant blend. To increase the challenge, each puzzle row has one or more letters that complete all but one of the words.

On the last page of this book, students can have fun writing sentences in which all or most of the words start with the same letter.

CLUELESS CROSSWORDS

Here is a high-challenge crossword puzzle variation in which there are no written clues to use in solving the puzzles. Instead, students fill in letters that form known words going both across and down.

Sometimes more than one letter is missing in a word, and sometimes more than two words are involved in determining the right missing letters. In almost all cases, several or more letters work going in one direction, but only one letter works going in both directions. As in many of the mini-books, the last two puzzles are the hardest. Be sure students use pencils with erasers!

Secret Codes

CRACK THE CODE

Students love to crack secret codes! On each puzzle page, students must decode a group of theme-related words written in an alphabet code. Each puzzle page uses a different alphabet code. Advise students to start their decoding by filling in all known letters in each of the puzzle words. They should be cautioned to be sure that they put these and all other decoded letters on the correct blanks. Before students begin, you may want to review with them the directions on mini-book page two. Depending on the abilities of your class, it may be helpful to do a decoding puzzle together on the board. Here's one:

PANNW	g r e e n
PAJH	_ _ _ _
XAJWPN	_ _ _ _ _ _
YDAYUN	_ _ _ _ _ _
KUDN	_ _ _ _
HNUUXF	_ _ _ _ _ _
KAXFW	_ _ _ _ _

Answers: gray, orange, purple, blue, yellow, brown

Antonyms & Synonyms

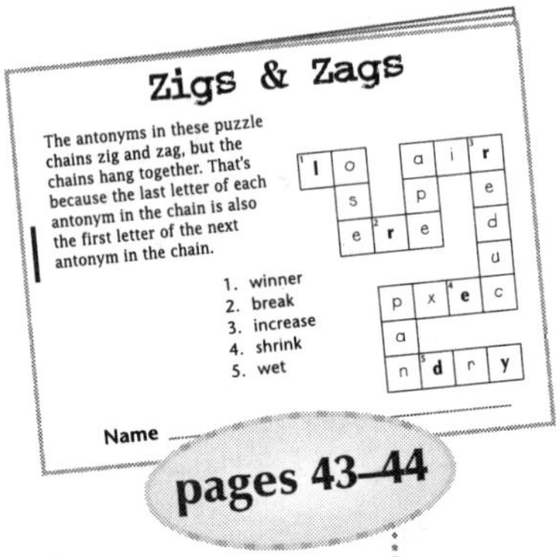

ZIGS & ZAGS

Students fill in antonyms for given words as they zig and zag their way through this unique puzzle format. The first and last letter of each antonym is given.

SYNONYM SEARCH

In this word search puzzle variation, students don't look for the words in the word list. Instead, they find a synonym for each of the listed words. Also hiding in the grids are antonyms for a few of the words on the list.

Making Words

SHRINK 'EMS

In these puzzles, students start with a five-letter word, shrink it down to a four-letter word, then a three-letter word and, finally, a two-letter word.

Many of the Shrink 'Ems have multiple answer possibilities. However, pages 6 and 7 present added challenges. Students must choose a four-letter word and then a three-letter word from which the given two-letter word can be made. Students may find that they've made a word from which another word can't be made. (For example, if students shrink the word "floor" to "fool," they'll be stuck and will have to start over again.)

BE A WORD WIZARD

Can your students change a reptile into a fish? Can they change a bird into a farm animal? To be "word wizards," students make a series of new words that match clues, changing just one letter each time. This mini-book includes a two-player game for more "word wizardry" fun. (Students might enjoy learning that this puzzle format was invented by Lewis Carroll, author of *Alice in Wonderland.* He called his puzzles "doublets." They first appeared in 1879 in the magazine *Vanity Fair.*)

Now try to find the **insects** that are in these words. Fill in the missing insect names to complete the words that fit the clues.

a kind of meat: ___ ___ ___ f

a piece of pizza or bread: s ___ ___ ___ ___

a doe to its fawn: ___ ___ ___ ___ e r

an old-fashioned vehicle: ___ ___ ___ g y

you need one to see a movie: ___ ___ ___ ___ e t

butterflies have them: ___ ___ ___ e n n a e

6

Rats!

Is that a rat in the refrigerator? Fill in the missing letters to complete the "ratty" words that fit these clues.

a baby's toy: r a t ___ ___ ___

Captain Hook was one: ___ ___ r a t ___

something to do if you itch: ___ ___ r a t ___ ___

98.6°F, for example: ___ ___ ___ ___ ___ r a t ___ ___ ___

some birds do this for the winter: ___ ___ ___ r a t ___

Super Stumper:
a long outdoor foot race: ___ ___ r a t ___ ___ ___

3

Which **mammal** is in each of these words? Fill in the missing mammal names to complete the words that fit the clues.

a large number: m i l ___ ___ ___ ___

Santa has a white one: ___ ___ ___ ___ d

a type of boat: k a ___ ___ ___

a source of power: ___ ___ ___ t e r y

a kind of fruit: g r ___ ___ ___

a week at the beach, for example: v a ___ ___ ___ i o n

8

There's a Bird in That Word

Q. What's an owl's favorite sport?

A. B owl i n g

Name ______________________

There are **farm animals** in these words. Can you fill in the missing letters to complete the words that fit the clues?

an opposite of "older": ___ e w e ___

an ancient Egyptian structure: ___ ___ r a m ___ ___

an organ of the body: k i d ___ ___ ___

someone who's not very brave: c o w ___ ___ ___

a bird seen in city parks: p i g ___ ___ ___

Super Stumper:
it's used for jumping fun: ___ r a m ___ ___ ___ ___ ___ ___ ___

4

Did you see the **ant** in the restaurant? Fill in the missing letters to complete the words that fit the clues.

male deer have them: a n t ___ ___ ___ ___

this mammal has a trunk: ___ ___ ___ ___ ___ a n t

a synonym for "baby": ___ ___ ___ a n t

5

Birds are hiding in these words! Can you fill in the missing letters to complete the words that fit the clues?

it's filled with air: ___ ___ ___ l o o n

a kind of tool : w r e n ___ ___

an angry look: ___ ___ o w l

a room in a house: ___ ___ ___ ___ h e n

to feel sorry: ___ e g r e t

a type of oven: ___ ___ c r o w ___ ___ ___

2

What **adjective** describes a fish that won't share?

___ ___ ___ f i s h

Here are more words in which there are ocean dwellers. Fill in the missing letters to complete the words that fit the clues.

it's followed by an "!": ___ ___ c l a m ___ ___ ___ ___ ___

a reptile: ___ ___ ___ c o d ___ ___ ___

a type of metal: ___ ___ e e l

7

Wordy Wigglers

The "caterpillars" in this mini-book are packed with overlapping words and words within words. All of the words are formed with letters that are next to each other.

Can you find 18 words with three or more letters in this Wordy Wiggler?

Name ______________________

fall, all, less, son, lesson, song, glove, love, over, very, you, your, our, rod, rode, rodent, den, dent

There are 17 **words** with three or more letters in this Wordy Wiggler.

b a d d r e s s h i p l a n e t r i m a s k i p

There are 19 **words** with three or more letters in this Wordy Wiggler.

r o t a t e a c h a n g e r m o t h e r i p e t

There are 18 **words** with three or more letters in this Wordy Wiggler.

s p i l l o w a s t a r r o w h e a t a p e e l

There are 18 **words** with three or more letters in this Wordy Wiggler.

i f o r t u n e a r t h i n k n o w i n d o w n

There are 18 **words** with three or more letters in this Wordy Wiggler.

s p i t c h a i r i b b o n e g g o l d r a g e

There are 17 **words** with three or more letters in this Wordy Wiggler.

s h o w h o l e m o n e y e t h i s l i d e a r

There are 17 **words** with three or more letters in this Wordy Wiggler.

s c a r t o o n i c e n t e r u s h e l f i n d

The Case of the Mis"{Poof}"Words

The word "sing" in "missing" is missing. In fact, lots of words are missing in this mini-book.

Name ____________________

Correctly complete each word below by inserting one of the words that is under the magnifying glass.

Answer Words

bed
tree
hear
lap
rib
harm
dent
miss

ter ________ le
p ________ acy
re ________ sal
per ________ ion
col ________ se
i ________ ical
o ________ ient
s ________ t

3

Correctly complete each word below by inserting one of the words that is under the magnifying glass.

Answer Words

side
very
iron
over
ever
time
end
gum

s ________ al
g ________ nment
ar ________ ent
con ________ r
cen ________ ter
env ________ ment
fri ________
bra ________

6

Correctly complete each word below by inserting one of the words that is under the magnifying glass.

Answer Words

opera
log
ill
ogre
our
right
ounce
ice

ann ________
ju ________
v ________ ain
pr ________ ss
c ________ tesy
co ________ te
apo ________ ize
f ________ en

8

Correctly complete each word below by inserting one of the words that is under the magnifying glass.

Answer Words

sure
cell
name
jam
star
crop
fin
fun

_______ ction
or _______ nt
mi _______ hone
ex _______ ent
pa _______ as
mea _______ ment
mu _______ d
de _______ ite

Correctly complete each word below by inserting one of the words that is under the magnifying glass.

Answer Words

pear
ratio
car
pet
ton
actor
tin
path

ap _______ ite
f _______ y
deco _______ n
sym _______ y
ma _______ oni
ap _______ ance
ex _______ ct
as _______ ish

Correctly complete each word below by inserting one of the words that is under the magnifying glass.

Answer Words

mend
live
tell
chase
chin
quit
chest
anger

or _______ ra
mos _______ o
de _______ ry
d _______ ous
cons _______ ation
pur _______
ma _______ ery
tre _______ ous

Correctly complete each word below by inserting one of the words that is under the magnifying glass.

Answer Words

last
rough
use
rag
sign
liar
fur
race

_______ ious
th _______
pecu _______
de _______ er
g _______ ful
m _______ um
f _______ ile
p _______ ic

Mussels With Muscles

"Mussel" and "muscle" are homonyms—words that sound the same but have different spellings and meanings.

Name ____________________

Write in the word that fits the pair of definitions. Each answer is a word that has the same spelling but two or more different meanings.

It's a name for a container with a lip for pouring.
It's also the name for a position on a baseball team.

____

As a noun, it's a term for animal skin.
As a verb, it's a synonym for "conceal."

____

It's a term for a unit of weight.
It also means "to strike or hit with heavy blows."

____

Answer each of these riddles with a pair of **homonyms**. Remember: Homonyms are words that sound the same but have different spellings and meanings.

What do you call seven days with no strength?

a w ___ ___ ___ w ___ ___ ___

What do you call a female relative of a tiny insect?

an ___ ___ t's ___ ___ ___ t

What do you call an amphibian being pulled on a rope?

a t ___ ___ ___ ___ t ___ ___ ___

What do you call a spicy, cold Mexican food?

c h ___ ___ ___ ___ c h ___ ___ ___

Illustrate two different meanings of one of these words:

box
fly
fence
palm
bat
pupil
bowl

Answer each of these riddles with a pair of **homonyms**.

What do you call a grizzly that's lost its fur?

a b ___ ___ ___ b ___ ___ ___

How do you start a letter to an animal with antlers?

D ___ ___ ___ d ___ ___ ___

What did they call the armored soldier who guarded the castle from 8:00 P.M. to 5:00 A.M.?

the ___ ___ ___ ___ t ___ ___ ___ ___ ___ t

Write in the **word** that fits the pair of definitions.

It's a term for one of four equal parts. It's also the name of an American coin.

____

As an adjective, it describes someone who waits without complaining. As a noun, it's a person receiving medical treatment.

____

It's the name for something used to create a cool breeze. It also means "an enthusiastic admirer."

____

Answer each of these riddles with a pair of **homonyms**.

What do you call a farm animal with a husky voice?

a h ___ ___ ___ ___ ___ h ___ ___ ___ ___

What do you call an undecorated jet?

a p ___ ___ ___ ___ p ___ ___ ___ ___

What do you call a penny that's been mailed?

a ___ ___ ___ t ___ ___ ___ t

Write in the **word** that fits the pair of definitions.

It's a term for land on the sides of a river. It's also the name for a place where money earns interest.

____

As a noun, it's a compartment in a stable. As a verb, it means "to use excuses to delay doing something."

____

It's a term for a level or floor of a building. It's also the name for a tale or an account of an event.

____

Use a prefix or a suffix to change each underlined word. Then put each numbered letter on the correct line at bottom.

a female lion ___ ___ ___ ___ ___ ___(8) ___

someone who is visiting ___ ___ ___ ___ ___ ___ ___(3)

the opposite of "correct" ___(5) ___ ___ ___ ___ ___ ___ ___ ___

describing someone stronger than others ___ ___ ___ ___ ___ ___ ___(2) ___ ___(6)

things used by someone who is equipped ___ ___ ___ ___ ___ ___(4) ___(7) ___ ___(1)

What insect group in the tropics lives in a structure that can be over 20 feet high and have chimneys?

___(1) ___(2) ___(3) ___(4) ___(5) ___(6) ___(7) ___(8)

6

Use a prefix or a suffix to change each underlined word. Then put each numbered letter on the correct line at bottom.

describing someone who keeps secrets ___ ___ ___ ___ ___ ___ ___ ___ ___(6)

it's ruled by a king ___ ___ ___ ___ ___ ___(3) ___

someone who plays the violin ___ ___ ___ ___ ___ ___ ___ ___(1) ___

to cook ahead of time ___(2) ___ ___ ___ ___ ___ ___

the opposite of "changed" ___ ___(4) ___ ___ ___ ___ ___(5) ___ ___

What sea creature has no heart, no lungs, no brain and no mouth?

a/an ___(1) ___(2) ___(3) ___(4) ___(5) ___(6)

3

Use a prefix or a suffix to change each underlined word. Then put each numbered letter on the correct line at bottom.

describing someone who has hope ___ ___ ___ ___ ___(1) ___ ___(6)

the feeling of being happy ___ ___ ___ ___ ___ ___(4) ___ ___ ___(9)

it's shown by someone who's brave ___ ___ ___ ___ ___ ___(2) ___

something in which to compete ___ ___ ___ ___ ___ ___ ___ ___(5) ___ ___(3) ___

to make someone feel fright ___ ___ ___ ___(8) ___ ___ ___(7) ___

Where are a cricket's ears?

on its ___(1) ___(2) ___(3) ___(4) ___(5) ___(6) ___(7) ___(8) ___(9)

8

That's Amazing!

Q. How does the archerfish catch the insects it eats?

A. It squirts a powerful stream of well-aimed drops of water at its prey. When the insect falls into the water, the archerfish eats it. It can shoot water more than 3 feet into the air. For more amazing facts, turn the page.

Name ______________________

Use a prefix or a suffix to change each underlined word to a new word that fits the clue. Then put each numbered letter on the line with the same number at the bottom of the page.

someone who performs <u>magic</u> __ __ __ __ __ __ __(3) __(9)

the opposite of "<u>care</u>ful" __ __ __ __ __(6) __(5) __ __

someone who acts like a <u>fool</u> __ __ __ __ __ __ __(2)

the opposite of "<u>possible</u>" __ __(4) __ __ __ __ __ __ __ __(7)

someone who acts like a <u>hero</u> __ __ __ __(8) __ __(1)

What reptile can look forward and backward at the same time? __(1) __(2) __(3) __(4) __(5) __(6) __(7) __(8) __(9)

4

Use a prefix or a suffix to change each underlined word to a new word that fits the clue. Then put each numbered letter on the line with the same number at the bottom of the page.

to <u>heat</u> again __ __(3) __ __ __ __

it's formed when a person <u>perspire</u>s __ __ __ __ __ __ __ __(6) __ __ __ __(7)

the opposite of "<u>legal</u>" __ __(2) __ __ __ __ __

someone who <u>reside</u>s in a place __ __ __ __ __ __(1) __ __(8)

a quality shown by a <u>leader</u> __ __ __ __ __ __ __ __(5) __ __(4)

What mammal baby spends almost two years inside its mother before it's born? a/an __(1) __(2) __(3) __(4) __(5) __(6) __(7) __(8)

5

Use a prefix or a suffix to change each underlined word to a new word that fits the clue. Then put each numbered letter on the line with the same number at the bottom of the page.

something that is <u>invent</u>ed i n v e n t i o(4) n

in a <u>loud</u> way __ __ __ __ __(2) __

the opposite of "<u>agree</u>" __(5) __ __ __ __ __ __ __

describing something containing <u>poison</u> __ __ __ __ __ __ __(3) __ __

a temperature below <u>zero</u> __ __ __(1) __ __ __ __

What does a horned toad shoot from its eyes when it feels threatened? __(1) __(2) __(3) __(4) __(5)

2

Use a prefix or a suffix to change each underlined word to a new word that fits the clue. Then put each numbered letter on the line with the same number at the bottom of the page.

someone who <u>run</u>s __ __ __ __ __(7) __(2)

a shape with three <u>angle</u>s __(5) __ __ __ __ __ __ __

the opposite of "<u>behave</u>" __ __ __(4) __ __ __ __ __ __

a move from front to <u>back</u> __ __ __ __ __(1) __ __ __

something that can <u>break</u> __ __ __ __ __ __ __ __(6) __(3)

What do male monitor lizards often do at the start of mating season to attract a female?

__(1) __(2) __(3) __(4) __(5) __(6) __(7)

7

Rhyme Finds

In these word search puzzles, you need to find the words that rhyme with a given word. But watch out! Not all words that rhyme have endings that look alike.

Example

I heard a bird say a word. How absurd!

And . . . some words with the same endings don't rhyme.

I heard he grew a beard.

Name ____________________

Find and circle 17 words of three or more letters that rhyme with "**true.**"

w	v	i	e	w	h	s	e	w
e	o	o	z	e	c	l	u	e
n	s	d	r	e	w	h	y	l
e	o	h	s	t	o	o	t	b
m	w	e	u	f	c	w	h	o
g	e	b	l	u	e	e	y	t
l	r	c	u	v	b	l	o	w
u	h	w	e	r	g	f	u	o
e	t	h	r	o	u	g	h	m

3

Find and circle 16 words of four or more letters that rhyme with "**crate.**"

t	i	a	w	d	s	e	a	t
m	a	t	e	r	o	t	e	h
t	v	e	b	a	n	a	t	g
a	s	k	a	t	e	d	a	i
e	m	o	i	e	c	a	g	e
r	e	y	t	f	a	t	e	r
g	a	e	t	a	t	s	u	f
s	t	r	a	i	g	h	t	w
p	l	a	t	e	e	t	a	h

6

A hog and a frog
tripped over a log
when they tried to jog
with a dog in the fog.

Create rhymes with your rhyme finds. On a separate sheet of paper, make a list of all the rhyming words you found in one of the puzzles in this mini-book. Then write a poem using some of these rhyming words. Or use as many of these rhyming words as you can in a silly sentence.

8

Find and circle 16 words of four or more letters that rhyme with **"near."**

w	e	a	r	r	e	e	h	c
r	e	n	a	a	i	r	d	s
a	s	t	e	e	r	b	e	p
e	m	r	d	g	r	e	e	h
y	i	a	j	f	e	a	r	e
r	a	e	p	s	t	r	a	r
e	s	h	e	e	r	o	i	e
a	w	x	s	m	e	a	r	f
r	a	e	l	c	p	i	e	r

4

Find and circle 20 words of three or more letters that rhyme with **"sly."**

s	i	g	h	t	h	e	y	e
y	v	f	o	g	u	y	h	m
l	e	r	y	r	c	o	s	t
f	i	y	w	l	t	r	y	h
w	t	n	h	i	y	r	d	i
e	e	i	d	e	w	h	u	g
i	b	k	e	y	s	p	y	h
g	u	o	x	h	a	d	y	e
h	y	k	s	w	p	i	e	d

5

Find and circle 15 words of four or more letters that rhyme with **"score."** The first three are done for you.

f	c	h	o	r	e	f	d	k
l	b	o	e	v	r	u	o	f
o	o	u	r	a	o	r	o	y
o	r	r	o	g	h	u	r	s
r	e	r	t	c	s	o	t	n
e	r	u	h	l	m	s	o	o
t	o	o	s	o	a	r	u	r
i	m	p	o	r	e	h	r	e
v	d	w	o	r	e	r	o	s

2

Find and circle 16 words of three or more letters that rhyme with **"grow."**

d	l	o	g	w	o	r	c	g
a	o	b	c	o	f	u	o	e
w	h	o	o	h	w	o	m	o
e	p	w	w	s	a	w	t	h
s	a	k	n	o	w	o	o	d
n	r	i	h	l	g	n	w	o
e	f	o	w	e	m	s	s	u
w	e	o	t	u	d	o	e	g
b	l	o	w	t	o	u	g	h

7

Scary Harry's Haunted House

Unscramble each word below to find five creepy things you'll see in this haunted house. Then arrange the letters you put in the circles to find one more bone-chilling surprise.

s h o g t

c a b k l a c t

w o b b e c

h w c i t

n o m r e t s

6

Paws & Claws Pet Shop

Unscramble each word below to find five pets you'll see at this shop. Then arrange the letters you put in the circles to find one more of this shop's pets.

k n e s a

z i d l a r

r a s t m e h

p p u y p

h i f s g l o d

3

Ma and Pa Plunket's Farm

Unscramble each word below to find five things you'll see at this farm. Then arrange the letters you put in the circles to find one more farm sight.

c o r t r a t

b l a t e s

y a h n o w g a

n i k c h e c p o c o

c h a r d o r

8

Field Trip Scramble

These puzzles will take you on seven field trip adventures. So hop on the bus and bring your scrambled word skills! The names of what you'll see on each of these trips have been jumbled.

Name ____________________

Tilly's Totally Fresh Fruit Stand

Unscramble each word below to find five fruits you'll see (and maybe eat) at Tilly's fruit stand. Then arrange the letters you put in the circles to find one more tasty fruit.

m o n e l ___ ___ ___ ◯ ◯

p a g r e s ◯ ___ ___ ___ ___ ___

p a e h c ___ ◯ ___ ___ ___

r e r h y c ___ ___ ___ ___ ◯ ___

a b a n n a ___ ___ ___ ___ ___ ◯

◯◯◯◯◯◯

4

African Wildlife Safari

Unscramble each word below to find five mammals you'll see on this trip. Then arrange the letters you put in the circles to find one more safari sight.

e f f a r i g ◯ ___ ___ ___ ___ ___ ___

o n i l ◯ ___ ◯ ___

d a r p o e l ◯ ___ ___ ___ ___ ___ ___

r e z a b ___ ___ ___ ◯ ◯

p o p i h ___ ◯ ___ ___ ___

◯◯◯◯◯◯◯

5

Mega Metropolis, U.S.A.

Unscramble each word below to find five things you'll see in this very large city. Then arrange the letters you put in the circles to find one more of this big city's sights.

r a k p ___ ◯ ___ ___

b u y s a w ◯ ___ ___ ___ ___ ___

o l t e h ___ ___ ◯ ◯ ___

m u m u e s ___ ◯ ___ ___ ___ ___

x i a t ◯ ___ ___ ___

◯◯◯◯◯◯

2

Coral Reef Aquarium

Unscramble each word below to find five ocean dwellers you'll see in the tanks. Then arrange the letters you put in the circles to find one more of the aquarium's attractions.

d i s u q ___ ___ ◯ ___ ___

b r a c ◯ ___ ___ ___

r e s t b o l ___ ◯ ___ ___ ◯ ___ ___

g o n s e p ___ ___ ◯ ___ ___ ___

p r i h m s ◯ ___ ___ ___ ___ ◯

◯◯◯◯◯◯◯

7

Magic Hat Trick

Put just one word into the magic hat.
Presto Change-o! Ka-Zoom! Ka-Zam!
Incredible! Out come two new words.

Name ______________________

Try the magic hat trick on each word below. Using each letter in the word just once, make two new words—one two-letter word and one three-letter word.

faint	__ __	__ __ __
maple	__ __	__ __ __
groan	__ __	__ __ __
spine	__ __	__ __ __
bribe	__ __	__ __ __
tooth	__ __	__ __ __

3

Try the magic hat trick on each word below. Using each letter in the word just once, make two new words—one two-letter word and one three-letter word.

point	__ __	__ __ __
frame	__ __	__ __ __
fruit	__ __	__ __ __
brace	__ __	__ __ __
whole	__ __	__ __ __
guest	__ __	__ __ __

6

Try the magic hat trick on each word below. Using each letter in the word just once, make two new words—one two-letter word and one three-letter word.

wheat	__ __	__ __ __
broad	__ __	__ __ __
money	__ __	__ __ __
poise	__ __	__ __ __
gnome	__ __	__ __ __
alien	__ __	__ __ __

8

Try the magic hat trick on each word below. Using each letter in the word just once, make two new words—one two-letter word and one three-letter word.

field	__ __	__ __ __
shame	__ __	__ __ __
pupil	__ __	__ __ __
cheap	__ __	__ __ __
daisy	__ __	__ __ __
scout	__ __	__ __ __

4

Try the magic hat trick on each word below. Using each letter in the word just once, make two new words—one two-letter word and one three-letter word.

budge	__ __	__ __ __
wrote	__ __	__ __ __
tease	__ __	__ __ __
their	__ __	__ __ __
tunes	__ __	__ __ __
arise	__ __	__ __ __

5

Try the magic hat trick on each word below. Using each letter in the word just once, make two new words—one two-letter word and one three-letter word.

badly	b y	l a d
trade	__ __	__ __ __
mound	__ __	__ __ __
store	__ __	__ __ __
waist	__ __	__ __ __
beast	__ __	__ __ __

2

Try the magic hat trick on each word below. Using each letter in the word just once, make two new words—one two-letter word and one three-letter word.

boast	__ __	__ __ __
found	__ __	__ __ __
empty	__ __	__ __ __
burro	__ __	__ __ __
weird	__ __	__ __ __
spray	__ __	__ __ __

7

Chef Alfonso's Word Recipe

First, take a word—not too long and not too short. Put it into a large bowl. Next, add one letter. Then, stir and mix all the letters just so!

Fantastico! You've made a tasty new word.

Name ______________________________

Follow Chef Alfonso's recipe, adding the letter on the right to the word on the left.

turn + k ___ ___ ___ ___ ___

wave + e ___ ___ ___ ___ ___

rate + w ___ ___ ___ ___ ___

sift + r ___ ___ ___ ___ ___

fear + t ___ ___ ___ ___ ___

Super Stumper: Double the fun! Make two new words.

rose + h ___ ___ ___ ___ ___ ___ ___ ___ ___ ___

Follow Chef Alfonso's recipe, adding the letter on the right to the word on the left.

case + l ___ ___ ___ ___ ___

hens + i ___ ___ ___ ___ ___

barn + i ___ ___ ___ ___ ___

shoe + u ___ ___ ___ ___ ___

stir + w ___ ___ ___ ___ ___

Super Stumper: Double the fun! Make two new words.

worn + g ___ ___ ___ ___ ___ ___ ___ ___ ___ ___

Follow Chef Alfonso's recipe, adding the letter on the right to the word on the left.

hats + r ___ ___ ___ ___ ___

most + r ___ ___ ___ ___ ___

tire + g ___ ___ ___ ___ ___

wore + p ___ ___ ___ ___ ___

pale + p ___ ___ ___ ___ ___

Super Stumper: Double the fun! Make two new words.

cone + a ___ ___ ___ ___ ___ ___ ___ ___ ___ ___

Follow Chef Alfonso's recipe, adding the letter on the right to the word on the left.

near + l __ __ __ __ __

bear + v __ __ __ __ __

soil + p __ __ __ __ __

gift + h __ __ __ __ __

hope + n __ __ __ __ __

Super Stumper: Double the fun! Make two new words.

tore + w __ __ __ __ __ __ __ __ __ __

Follow Chef Alfonso's recipe, adding the letter on the right to the word on the left.

cane + l __ __ __ __ __

rags + s __ __ __ __ __

arch + i __ __ __ __ __

nose + r __ __ __ __ __

iron + h __ __ __ __ __

Super Stumper: Double the fun! Make two new words.

ache + t __ __ __ __ __ __ __ __ __ __

Follow Chef Alfonso's recipe, adding the letter on the right to the word on the left.

meal + t m e t a l

some + u __ __ __ __ __

chat + w __ __ __ __ __

male + c __ __ __ __ __

pond + u __ __ __ __ __

Super Stumper: Double the fun! Make two new words.

torn + h __ __ __ __ __ __ __ __ __ __

Follow Chef Alfonso's recipe, adding the letter on the right to the word on the left.

acre + m __ __ __ __ __

ripe + c __ __ __ __ __

meal + b __ __ __ __ __

sale + f __ __ __ __ __

cape + e __ __ __ __ __

Super Stumper: Double the fun! Make two new words.

hint + g __ __ __ __ __ __ __ __ __ __

Eating Your Words

To "eat your words" is an expression called an idiom. Idioms can't be taken literally. To understand them, you have to know their special meanings.

Lucy said we'd lose the game, but we won. Now she'll have to eat her words.

Name ______________________

Foods Complete each of these idioms by putting the name of a food on each blank. If you don't know the idiom, put in your best guess.

be a couch ______________ (sit around, be lazy)

walk on ______________ s (be very cautious)

in a ______________ (have a big problem)

spill the ______________ s (give away a secret)

a piece of ______________ (something that's very easy)

like two ______________ s in a pod (to be very similar)

go ______________ s (go crazy)

3

Similes Expressions that compare two things using the words "as" or "like" are called similes. Complete each of these popular similes by putting the name of an animal on each blank. If you don't know the simile, put in your best guess.

as wise as a/an __________

as proud as a/an __________

as sly as a/an __________

as busy as a/an __________

as graceful as a/an __________

as strong as a/an __________

as quiet as a/an __________

as stubborn as a/an __________

as gentle as a/an __________

6

Draw a picture that illustrates the meaning of one of the idioms in this mini-book. Write the idiom at the bottom of the page.

____

____

8

Animals Complete each of these idioms by putting the name of an animal on each blank. If you don't know the idiom, put in your best guess.

have a ________________ in your throat (be hoarse)

raining _____________ s and _____________ s (rain hard)

be a ________________ (feel fearful or anxious)

have ________________ s in your stomach (feel nervous)

________________ around (play noisily)

smell a ______________ (suspect something's wrong)

have ________s in your pants (feel restless)

Parts of the Body Complete each of the idioms on these two pages by putting the name of a part of the body on each blank. If you don't know the idiom, put in your best guess.

be all ________________ s (be eager to listen)

hold your ________________ (be silent)

have your _______________ in the clouds (to daydream)

make your ________________ water (look and smell tasty)

get it off your ________________ (make a confession)

get a pat on your ________________ (be praised)

make your ________________ stand on end (be scary)

be all ________________ s (be awkward or clumsy)

stick your ________________ out (take a risk)

button your ________________ (keep quiet)

pull someone's ________________ (fool someone)

catch your ________________ (be noticed)

on your ________________ s (be alert)

give someone a ________________ (help someone)

Create your own similes by completing each of the phrases below. Try to make your similes as descriptive as possible.

as funny as ____

as noisy as ____

as scary as ____

as fast as ____

as playful as ____

as angry as ____

fit	cycle	line	hall	flag	trip
motor	out	air	bell	way	pole
law	cap	side	knob	door	cone
burn	sun	walk	shoe	bone	pine
set	hot	shine	wish	fire	back

pen	play	hog	chair	high	window
stick	ground	wheel	arm	deep	way
yard	back	melon	lid	pit	drive
fall	water	brow	eye	ever	green
up	hot	ball	round	lash	house

weed	shell	shore	stage	dragon	hole
food	sea	sick	fly	coach	scotch
top	cave	fire	proof	hop	butter
sand	car	man	place	fruit	vine
mail	box	shade	lamp	apple	grape

Compound Roundup

Make as many compound words as you can by joining words in boxes that connect vertically, horizontally, or diagonally. Write your answers on a separate sheet of paper. **There are 20 compound words to round up in each puzzle**.

Name ______________________

pick	paste	ache	line	fore	over
drop	tooth	bird	head	how	moon
gum	cage	brush	some	light	saw
day	red	hair	thing	any	guard
home	dream	cut	body	life	where

cuffs	shake	wear	every	stand	drop
fog	hand	ship	under	rain	card
kick	horn	pants	bow	board	fold
drum	ache	time	black	cup	bill
ear	stick	lip	cake	spoon	tea

mill	wind	toe	tail	light	work
lady	bug	pig	pony	print	step
spread	bed	chop	class	mate	foot
tub	robe	room	stick	stool	mare
cold	bath	mush	way	time	night

skate	pull	quake	worm	pea	pit
board	over	blue	earth	suit	cock
surf	score	due	man	snow	case
bag	end	bench	see	storm	brief
week	bean	work	home	thing	brain

Put the correct missing word in the box and form two compound words—one with the word in front of the box and one with the word in back of the box.

base [ ] park

door [ ] ladder

sweat [ ] sleeves

gold [ ] hook

Super Stumper:

see [ ] horse [ ] lace

6

Put the correct missing word in the box and form two compound words—one with the word in front of the box and one with the word in back of the box.

touch [ ] stairs

bumble [ ] hive

tug [ ] house

tea [ ] holder

camp [ ] cracker

3

This time, fill in the missing letters to form eleven compound words that either end or begin with the word "book."

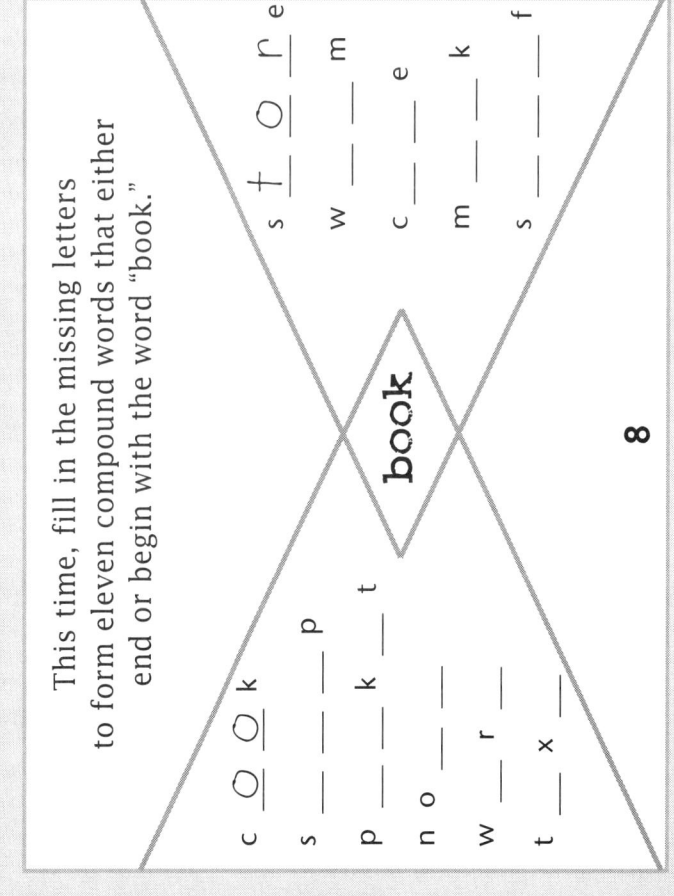

book

c o o k

s __ __ __ p

p __ __ k __ t

n o __ __

w __ r __

t __ x __

s t o r e

w __ __ m

c __ __ e

m __ __ k

s __ __ __ f

8

Barefoot Football

In these puzzles, you'll form pairs of compound words. Put the correct word in the box and you'll form two compound words—one with the word in front of the box and one with the word in back of the box.

Example:

bare [**foot**] **ball**

barefoot football

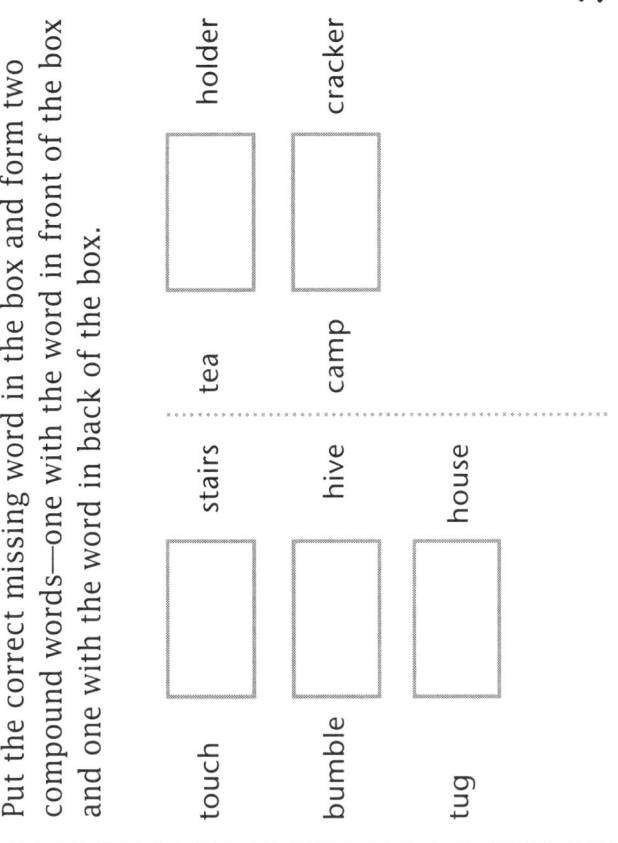

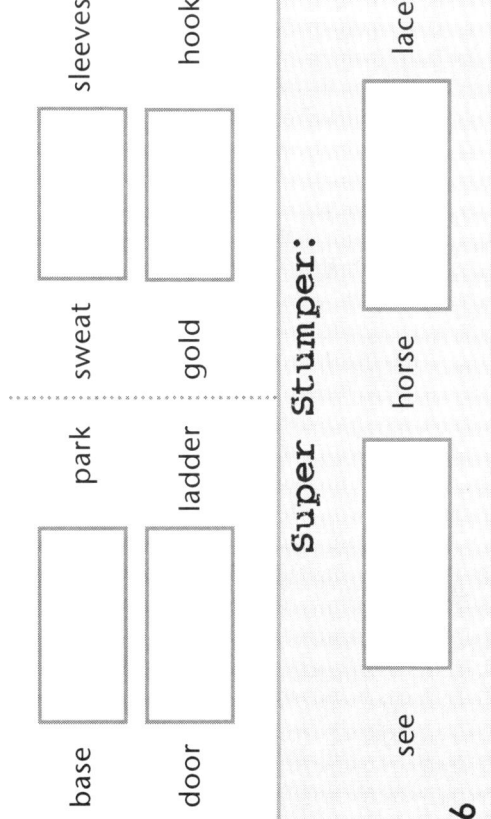

Name ________________

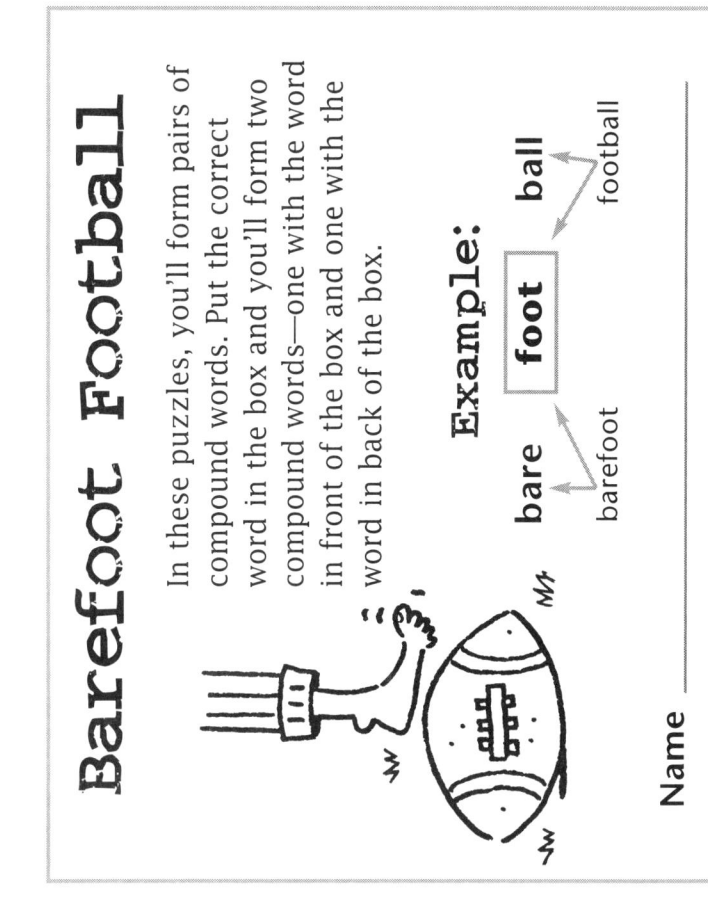

Put the correct missing word in the box and form two compound words—one with the word in front of the box and one with the word in back of the box.

jelly		bowl	news		weight
mid		gown	pea		cracker

Super Stumper:

pine		sauce		cake

Put the correct missing word in the box and form two compound words—one with the word in front of the box and one with the word in back of the box.

goal		card	tip		nail
battle		wreck	corn		web
turtle		tie			

Put the correct missing word in the box and form two compound words—one with the word in front of the box and one with the word in back of the box.

pop		stalk	birth		light
cow		friend	cart		barrow
waste		ball			

Put the correct missing word in the box and form two compound words—one with the word in front of the box and one with the word in back of the box.

quarter		pack	ear		master
scare		bar	ant		side
flash		house			

Put the correct syllables together to make six words.

mul	ni	cle	______________
bi	si	ply	______________
in	bi	ble	______________
mag	cy	tion	______________
sen	dus	fy	______________
am	ti	try	______________

6

Put the correct syllables together to make six words.

op	gi	saur	______________
ma	er	dar	______________
di	en	rine	______________
sub	fi	cian	______________
cal	no	ate	______________
of	ma	cer	______________

3

Put the correct syllables together to make six words.

or	ten	do	orchestra
an	ta	go	______________
fla	brel	tra	______________
um	na	to	______________
po	min	na	______________
tor	ches	la	______________

8

The Syllable Shuffler

Oh no! Snarg, the sly syllable shuffler, has played a pesky prank with the word lists in this mini-book. This sneaky prankster has mixed up the syllables and now none of the words make sense. Can you put the right syllables back together?

Name ______________________

Put the correct syllables together to make six words.

al	ro	teen	______
sev	sti	pal	______
ter	pha	ble	______
prin	en	tute	______
sub	ci	bat	______
ac	ri	bet	______

Put the correct syllables together to make six words.

de	rec	ment	______
gen	li	nate	______
hi	gu	cious	______
cor	er	dent	______
ac	ber	tion	______
ar	ci	ous	______

Put the correct syllables together to make six words.

rec	en	tic	rectangle
fan	cel	tine	______
ex	tan	ber	______
val	ven	gle	______
re	tas	ture	______
ad	mem	lent	______

Put the correct syllables together to make six words.

an	e	neer	______
rel	u	way	______
cel	i	tive	______
mon	y	ment	______
pi	a	nate	______
nom	o	brate	______

What's the missing consonant for each row? Fill in the blanks with the ONE letter that makes sense in all four words in the row.

1. ___all ___ale ___ummy bla___e
2. ___unk ___imple ___ull ___rown
3. ___old ___ail ___oof ___airy
4. ___ell wi___e ___ound ___udge

Super Stumper: Using just one letter, fill in the blanks and complete the word.

___a___ ___le___ale

What's the missing consonant for each row? Fill in the blanks with the ONE letter that makes sense in all four words in the row.

1. ___oot ___ake li___e ___eather
2. ___ill ___ink s___ell ___ocket
3. ___ive ___ate ___low ___rain
4. ___eal ___iddle ___ole ba___k

Super Stumper: Using just one letter, fill in the blanks and complete the word.

___a___ ___al

Elbert eats eight eel eggs every evening.

Try writing some sentences in which all (or almost all) of the words start with the same letter.

____

____

____

____

One for All

Fill in the blanks,
Just one letter will do.
Is it a "d", an "m" or a "q"?
It might be a "p",
But what is a "prew"?

___atch ___age ri___e ___rew

Do you know what ONE letter correctly completes each of these words?

Name ______________________________

What's the missing consonant for each row? Fill in the blanks with the ONE letter that makes sense in all four words in the row.

1.	c a ___ e	___ a v e	n o ___ e	___ i f t
2.	___ e n d	___ u n c h	___ i c k	f o o ___
3.	___ e n t	___ e a c h	___ o a d	___ r i m
4.	___ a n g	___ o r n	___ a n d	___ e e n

Super Stumper: Using just one letter, fill in the blanks and complete the word.

c ___ c ___ ___ n

4

What's the missing consonant for each row? Fill in the blanks with the ONE letter that makes sense in all four words in the row.

1.	___ a s h	___ e e p	___ a s t e	___ i r e
2.	___ u m p	___ i n t	___ i l e	s h o ___
3.	___ o n e	s ___ o r e	___ i c e	___ a m e
4.	___ o o k	m i ___ e	___ o u g h	___ l u e

Super Stumper: Using just one letter, fill in the blanks and complete the word.

p o ___ ___ e ___ ___ i o n

5

What's the missing consonant for each row? Fill in the blanks with the ONE letter that makes sense in all four words in the row.

1.	___ e a t	___ o s s	l a ___ e	___ a r k
2.	___ i n d	___ o o l	___ e e d	___ e e k
3.	m a ___ e	___ o o m	d o ___ e	s i ___ e
4.	___ e a d	___ u m b l e	___ e e l	___ i k e

Super Stumper: Using just one letter, fill in the blanks and complete the word.

___ u ___ ___ a b y

2

What's the missing consonant for each row? Fill in the blanks with the ONE letter that makes sense in all four words in the row.

1.	___ e s t	h e a ___	___ o s e	h i ___ e
2.	___ o v e	___ a w n	s ___ e e p	___ i m e
3.	___ a r e	___ a c k	___ o i l	___ l u s h
4.	___ o u r	___ o r e	___ a n k	l o ___ e

Super Stumper: Using just one letter, fill in the blanks and complete the word.

___ i ___ ___ l i n ___

7

Fill in the squares to complete the words in this puzzle. Be careful though, and have an eraser handy. Form words that make sense going both across and down. (No proper nouns, please.)

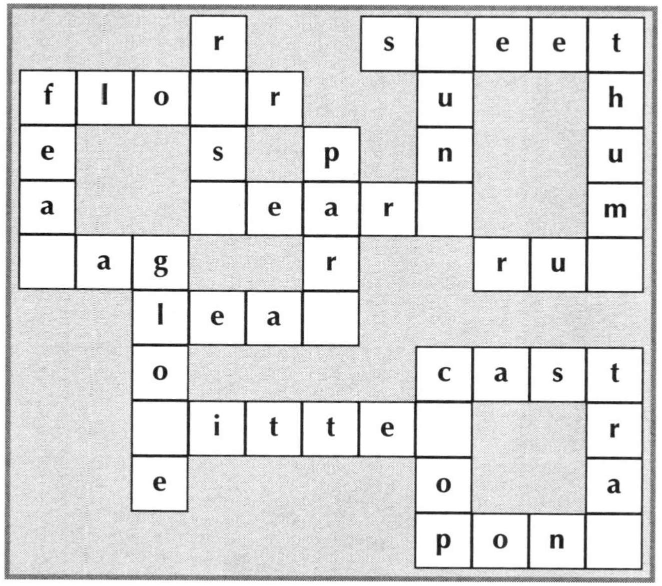

6

Fill in the squares to complete the words in this puzzle. Be careful though, and have an eraser handy. Form words that make sense going both across and down. (No proper nouns, please.)

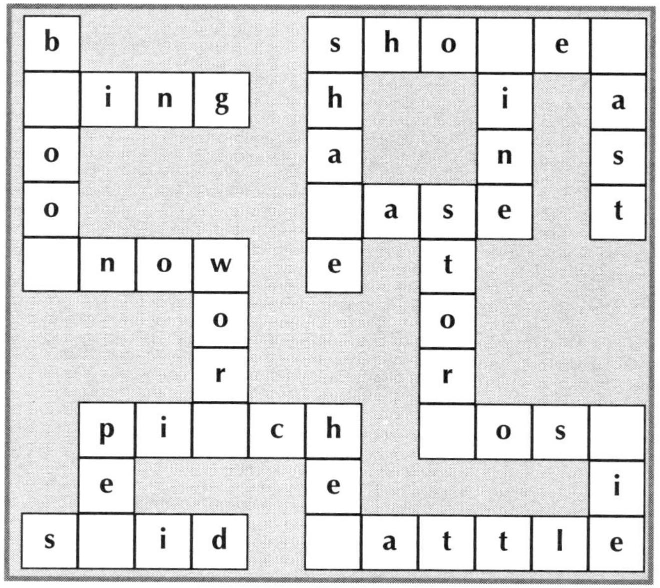

3

Fill in the squares to complete the words in this puzzle. Be careful though, and have an eraser handy. Form words that make sense going both across and down. (No proper nouns, please.)

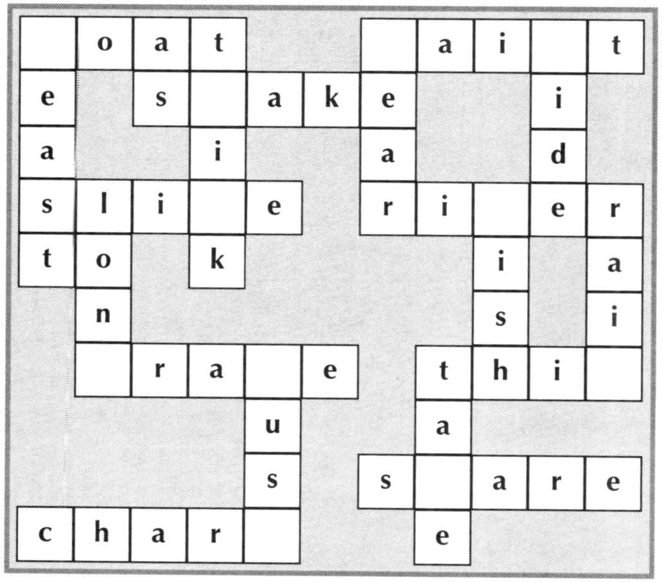

8

Clueless Crosswords

Can you complete the puzzle?

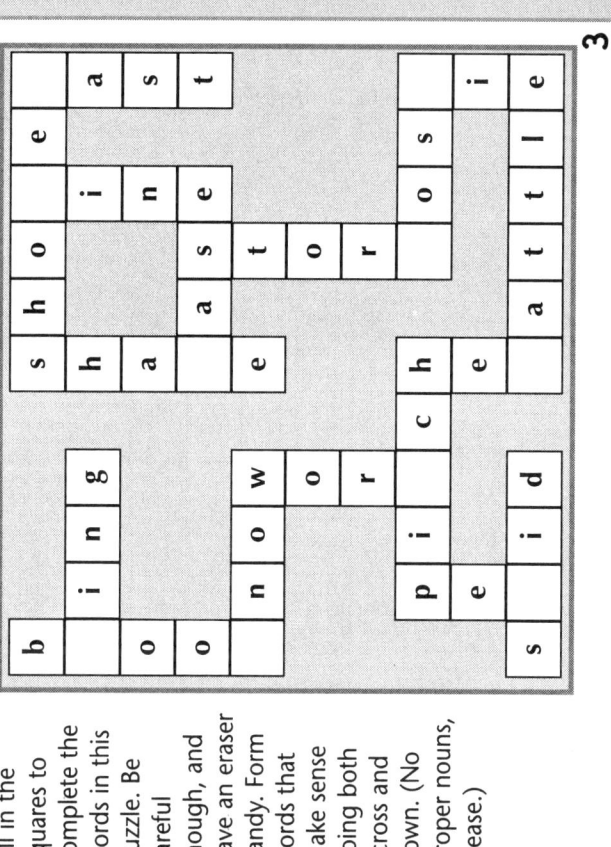

Name ______________________

Fill in the squares to complete the words in this puzzle. Be careful though, and have an eraser handy. Form words that make sense going both across and down. (No proper nouns, please.)

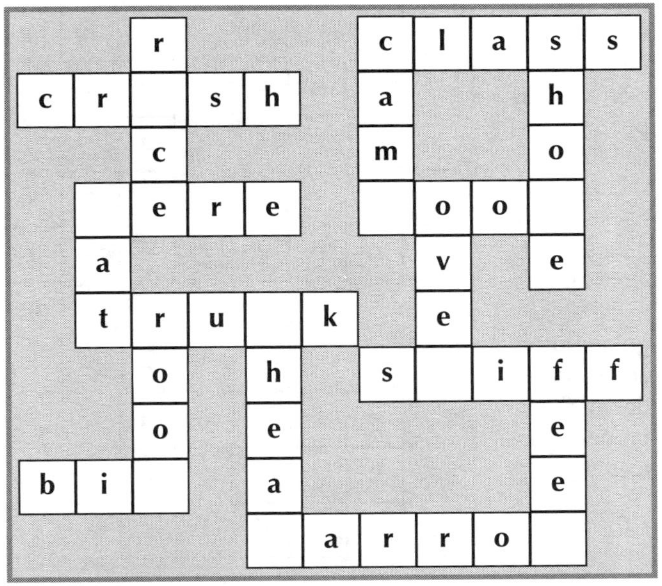

Fill in the squares to complete the words in this puzzle. Be careful though, and have an eraser handy. Form words that make sense going both across and down. (No proper nouns, please.)

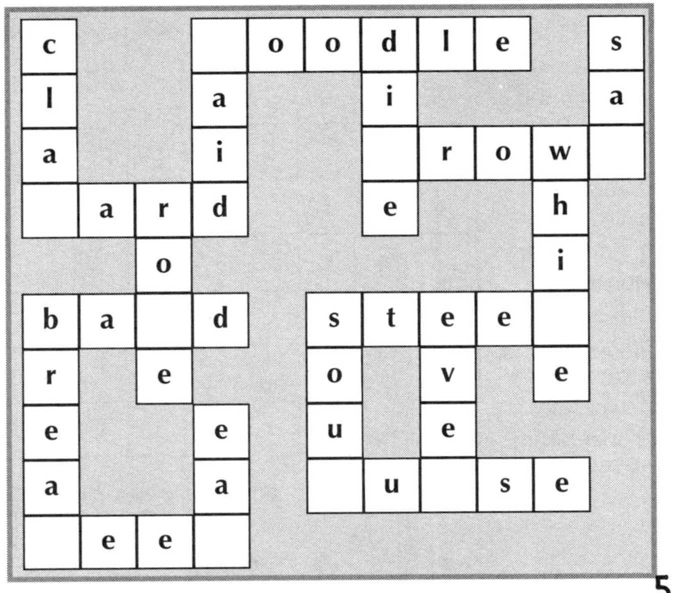

Fill in the squares to complete the words in this puzzle. Be careful though, and have an eraser handy. Form words that make sense going both across and down. (No proper nouns, please.)

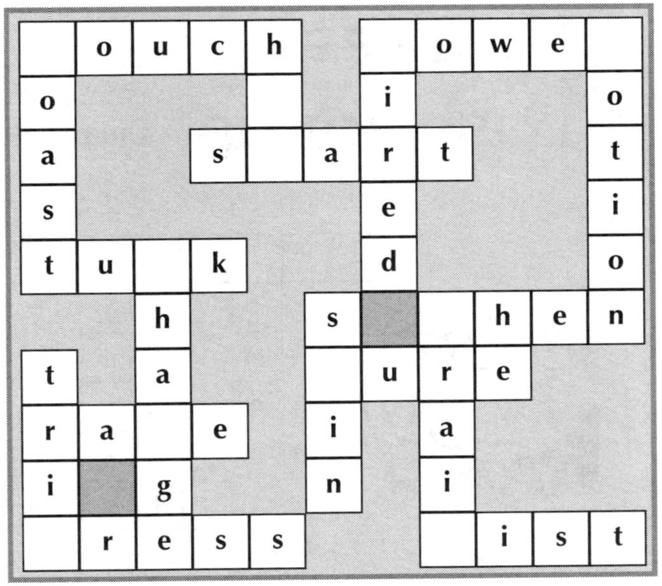

Fill in the squares to complete the words in this puzzle. Be careful though, and have an eraser handy. Form words that make sense going both across and down. (No proper nouns, please.)

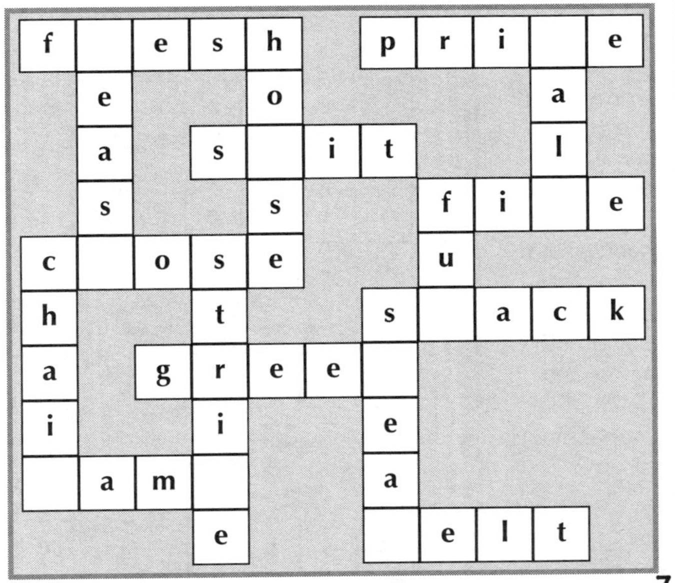

Crack the Code

On each page of this mini-book, a group of related words are written in an alphabet code. Here's "secret code" written in an alphabet code:

HVXIVG XLWV
secret code

Turn the page for code puzzle directions.

Name ______________________

Good Sports

Crack the code for this group of names of sports.

GTBQNSL b o w l i n g
GFXPJYGFQQ __ __ __ __ __ __ __ __ __ __
KTTYGFQQ __ __ __ __ __ __ __ __
YJSSNX __ __ __ __ __ __
XTHHJW __ __ __ __ __ __
PFWFYJ __ __ __ __ __ __
XBNRRNSL __ __ __ __ __ __ __ __

Get in Shape

Crack the code for this group of names of geometric shapes.

DEZFXASVL t r a p e z o i d
QFJXEX __ __ __ __ __ __
FNEZTVL __ __ __ __ __ __ __
QRPZEX __ __ __ __ __ __
YVEYHX __ __ __ __ __ __
YNHVGLXE __ __ __ __ __ __ __ __
FXGDZWSG __ __ __ __ __ __ __ __

What's My Job?

Crack the code for this group of names of occupations.

UDEFHPVZM p o l i c e m a n
UEBVQPC __ __ __ __ __ __ __
HZTOFPC __ __ __ __ __ __ __
EFQCZCFZM __ __ __ __ __ __ __ __ __
CPUDCKPC __ __ __ __ __ __ __ __
YDHKDC __ __ __ __ __ __
QBT YCFSPC __ __ __ __ __ __ __ __ __

Code Puzzle Directions

1. A new set of letters has been substituted for the correct letters in each group of related words.
2. The substituted letters remain the same in each word in the group. For example, if "R" represents "g" in one word, "R" will represent "g" in all words in the group
3. The first word in the group has been decoded for you. Write its decoded letters on the correct blanks in all of the words in which the same code letters appear.
4. Each new word and letter you decode will help you decode remaining coded words and letters.
5. Each new puzzle page uses a different alphabet code.

A hint: Use the subject of each word group to help you think of related words.

Sweet Treats Crack the code for this group of names of sweet things to eat.

OAAWUQE c o o k i e s

OGB OMWQ ___ ___ ___ ___ ___ ___ ___

UOQ ODQMY ___ ___ ___ ___ ___ ___ ___ ___

MBBXQ BUQ ___ ___ ___ ___ ___ ___ ___ ___

NDAIZUQ ___ ___ ___ ___ ___ ___ ___

YMDETYMXXAI ___ ___ ___ ___ ___ ___ ___ ___ ___ ___ ___

OTQDDK FMDF ___ ___ ___ ___ ___ ___ ___ ___ ___ ___

Weather Report Crack the code for this group of words related to weather.

PDQJZAN t h u n d e r

HECDPJEJC ___ ___ ___ ___ ___ ___ ___ ___ ___

DQNNEYWJA ___ ___ ___ ___ ___ ___ ___ ___ ___

YHKQZ ___ ___ ___ ___ ___

PKNJWZK ___ ___ ___ ___ ___ ___ ___

XHEVVWNZ ___ ___ ___ ___ ___ ___ ___ ___

NWEJOPKNI ___ ___ ___ ___ ___ ___ ___ ___ ___

Head to Toe Crack the code for this group of names of parts of the body.

LPKEPGKN v e r t e b r a

TXWOCP ___ ___ ___ ___ ___ ___

BPNKE ___ ___ ___ ___ ___

WEUTNOB ___ ___ ___ ___ ___ ___ ___

EBKUNE ___ ___ ___ ___ ___ ___

GKNRJ ___ ___ ___ ___ ___

GUJP ___ ___ ___ ___

Zigs & Zags

The antonyms in these puzzle chains zig and zag, but the chains hang together. That's because the last letter of each antonym in the chain is also the first letter of the next antonym in the chain.

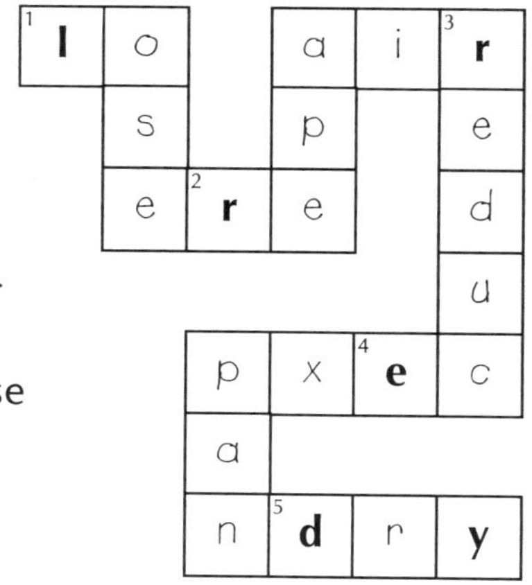

1. winner
2. break
3. increase
4. shrink
5. wet

Name ______________________

Complete the antonym for each word below. The last letter of each antonym is the first letter of the next antonym. So, in this chain, the first antonym ends with "l" in square 2.

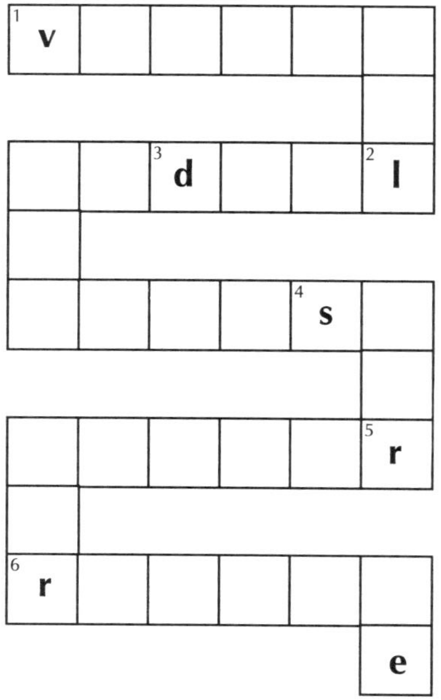

1. horizontal
2. quiet
3. safe
4. sweet
5. forget
6. give

Complete the antonym for each word below. The last letter of each antonym is the first letter of the next antonym. So, in this chain, the first antonym ends with "p" in square 2.

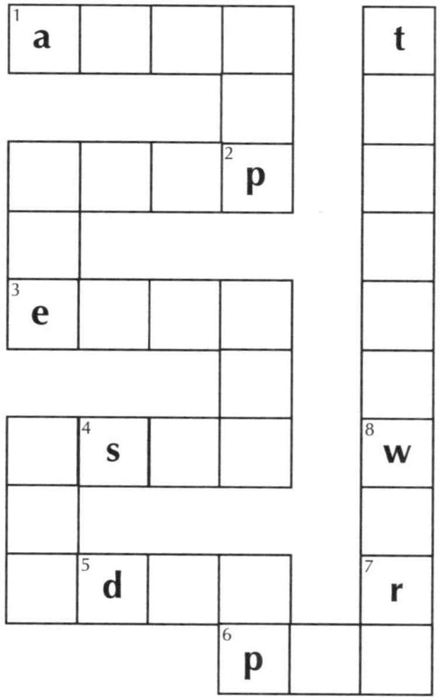

1. awake
2. rude
3. tiny
4. save
5. shallow
6. wealthy
7. cooked
8. strongest

Complete the antonym for each word below. The last letter of each antonym is the first letter of the next antonym. So, in this chain, the first antonym ends with "w" in square 2.

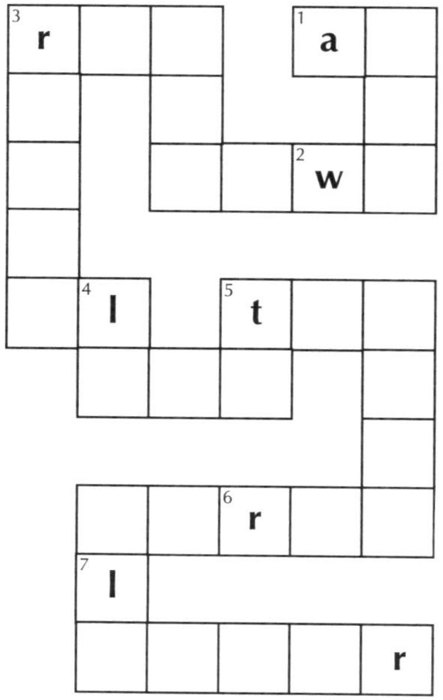

1. forbid
2. shout
3. conceal
4. most
5. alone
6. fake
7. follower

Complete the antonym for each word below. The last letter of each antonym is the first letter of the next antonym. So, in this chain, the first antonym ends with "n" in square 2.

1. answer
2. always
3. smooth
4. soft
5. shiny
6. truth
7. cheap
8. full

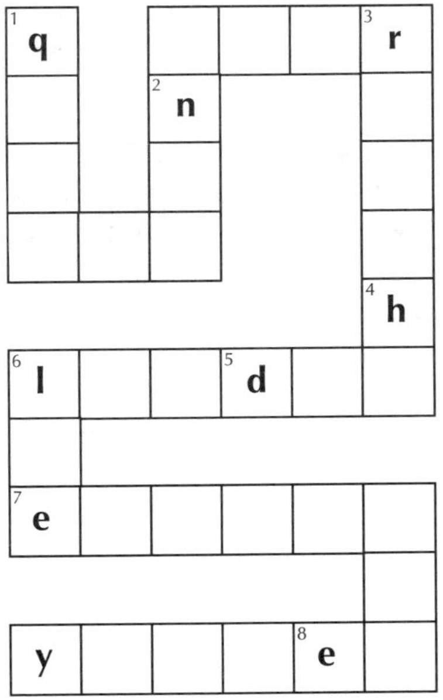

Complete the antonym for each word below. The last letter of each antonym is the first letter of the next antonym. So, in this chain, the first antonym ends with "d" in square 2.

1. backward
2. attack
3. same
4. catch
5. best
6. bottom
7. ashamed

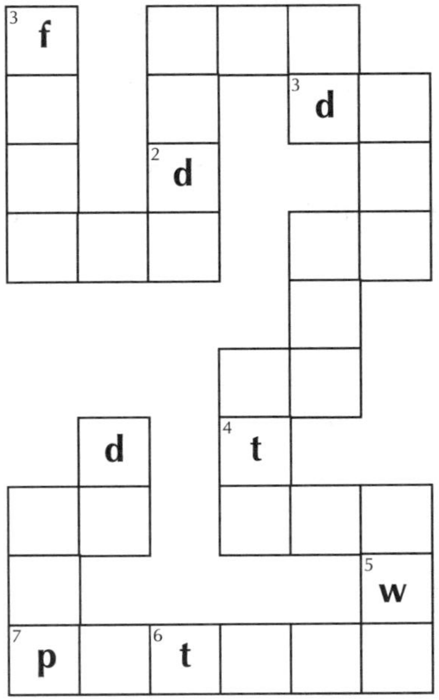

Complete the antonym for each word below. The last letter of each antonym is the first letter of the next antonym. So, in this chain, the first antonym ends with "h" in square 2.

1. wise
2. sick
3. old
4. selfish
5. float
6. cruel
7. arrive

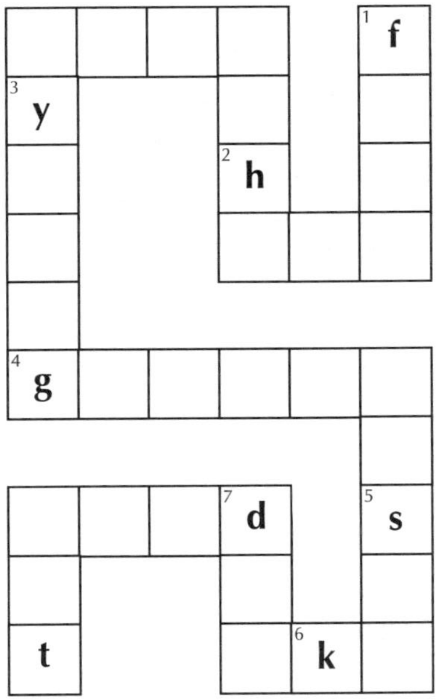

Complete the antonym for each word below. The last letter of each antonym is the first letter of the next antonym. So, in this chain, the first antonym ends with "t" in square 2.

1. guilty
2. wild
3. exit
4. odd
5. wide
6. east
7. thick
8. all

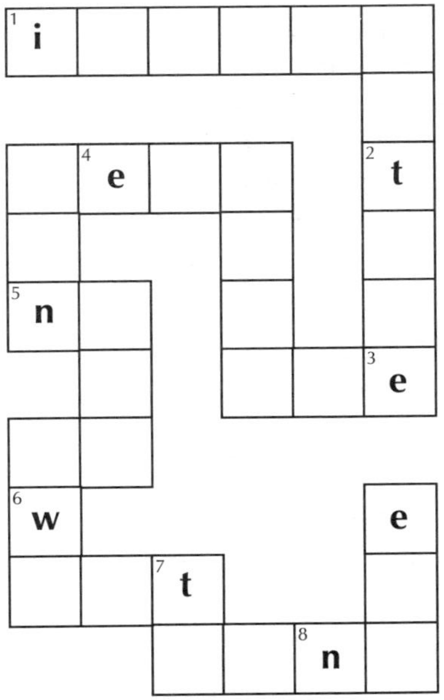

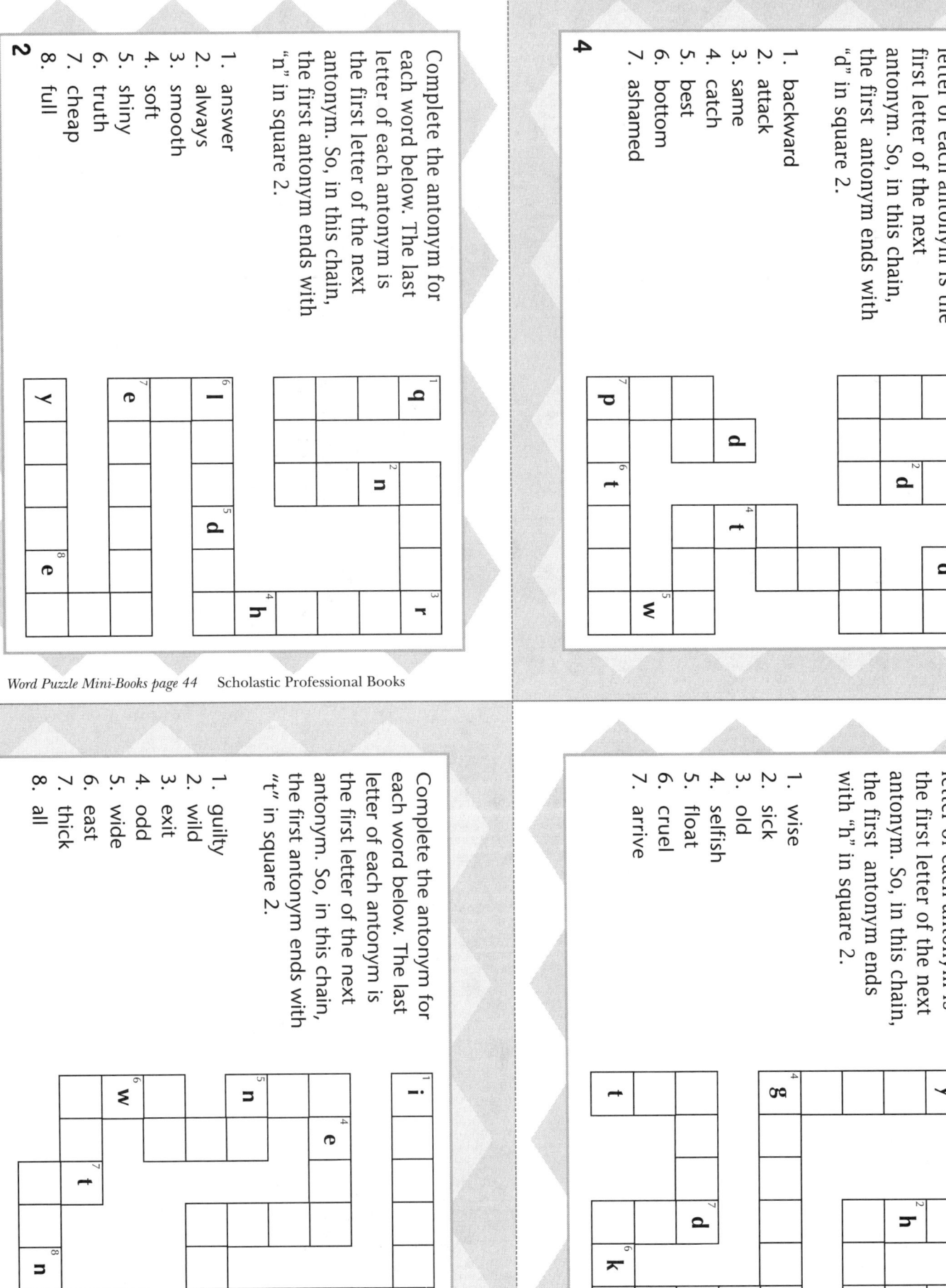

Synonym Search

Two or more words with the same or nearly the same meaning are called synonyms.

On each page, find and circle a synonym for each word on the list. Then write the synonym pairs on a separate sheet of paper. The letters of each synonym go forward across the square or down the square. Letters can be circled more than once.

He's *huge!*
Enormous!
Gigantic!
Immense!
Gargantuan!
Humongous!

Name ____________________

Word List

wealthy
mistake
convince
moist
terrible
acquire
bother
stay
brag
slender

s	h	e	d	a	m	p	e
t	e	r	r	o	r	e	f
r	p	e	g	e	t	r	a
a	o	m	b	o	a	s	t
w	o	a	m	t	n	u	g
f	r	i	c	h	n	a	o
u	l	n	e	i	o	d	o
l	d	r	y	n	y	e	d

Word List

almost
dodge
worth
beneath
permit
require
vacant
cross
secure
cry

c	h	a	n	g	r	y	t
h	a	l	l	o	w	v	h
a	v	o	n	s	e	a	e
s	o	o	e	a	e	l	m
e	i	s	e	f	p	u	p
a	d	e	d	e	m	e	t
b	o	n	e	a	r	l	y
s	u	n	d	e	r	t	h

Word List

faithful
capture
foe
conscious
entire
quarrel
numerous
destroy
possess
sloppy

g	l	o	w	n	e	s	t
s	c	a	t	c	h	l	a
a	m	a	n	y	e	o	r
w	e	r	p	a	l	y	g
a	s	u	f	e	w	a	u
r	s	i	w	h	o	l	e
e	y	n	o	n	e	a	t
d	e	n	e	m	y	e	t

Word List

find
awkward
assist
feeble
astonish
inquire
too
observe
dull
journey

s	w	e	a	k	i	s	s
t	c	b	a	s	k	h	l
r	l	o	c	a	t	e	o
o	u	r	o	l	r	l	w
n	m	i	s	s	i	p	a
g	s	n	h	o	p	e	t
e	y	g	l	o	s	e	c
t	a	m	a	z	e	k	h

4

Word List

purchase
final
applaud
decay
altitude
cost
harm
jump
disappear
attempt

t	v	a	n	i	s	h	o
p	i	t	c	h	b	u	y
r	l	s	l	e	p	t	m
i	e	e	a	i	a	r	a
c	a	l	p	g	t	y	d
e	p	l	c	h	u	r	t
p	l	a	s	t	o	n	e
f	i	n	d	r	o	t	e

5

Word List

weary
select
neat
construct
peculiar
courageous
center
connect
rush
thought

s	e	w	j	o	i	n	t
o	t	h	e	m	t	o	i
b	b	u	s	y	i	d	m
r	u	r	i	m	r	d	i
a	i	r	i	d	e	a	d
v	l	y	t	i	d	y	d
e	d	a	w	a	k	e	l
t	e	c	h	o	o	s	e

2

Word List

answer
frequently
tremble
certain
forgive
elevate
impolite
desire
wander
disregard

g	n	e	v	e	r	q	s
r	a	i	s	e	o	u	p
s	r	a	s	k	a	a	a
u	u	s	e	e	m	k	r
r	d	c	r	a	v	e	d
e	e	o	f	t	e	n	o
d	i	g	n	o	r	e	n
s	t	r	e	p	l	y	e

7

This time you've been given the final two-letter word. Choose a four-letter word and then a three-letter word from which this two-letter word can be made.

d r o w n
_ _ _ _
_ _ _
o r

m a r r y
_ _ _ _
_ _ _
m y

6

Take away one letter and use the remaining letters to make a four letter word. Repeat these steps to make a three-letter word and then a two-letter word.

s k u n k
_ _ _ _
_ _ _
_ _

w a t c h
_ _ _ _
_ _ _
_ _

3

Take away one letter and use the remaining letters to make a four letter word. Repeat these steps to make a three-letter word and then a two-letter word.

b e a r d
_ _ _ _
_ _ _
_ _

g r e a t
_ _ _ _
_ _ _
_ _

8

Shrink 'Ems

"I'm shrinking!" cried the *giant* as he became a *gnat* and then an *ant*.

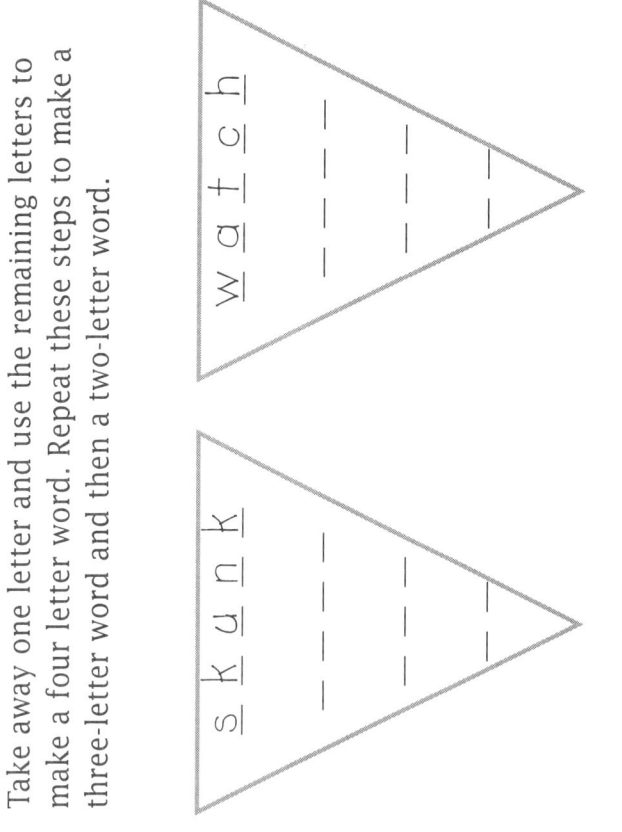

g i a n t
g n a t
a n t

Name ____________________

Take away one letter and use the remaining letters to make a four letter word. Repeat these steps to make a three-letter word and then a two-letter word.

f l o o r

_ _ _ _

_ _ _

_ _

s t e a m

_ _ _ _

_ _ _

_ _

4

Take away one letter and use the remaining letters to make a four letter word. Repeat these steps to make a three-letter word and then a two-letter word.

t o d a y

_ _ _ _

_ _ _

_ _

s w e e t

_ _ _ _

_ _ _

_ _

5

Take away one letter and use the remaining letters to make a four letter word. Repeat these steps to make a three-letter word and then a two-letter word.

c o u l d

_ _ _ _

_ _ _

_ _

o u n c e

_ _ _ _

_ _ _

_ _

2

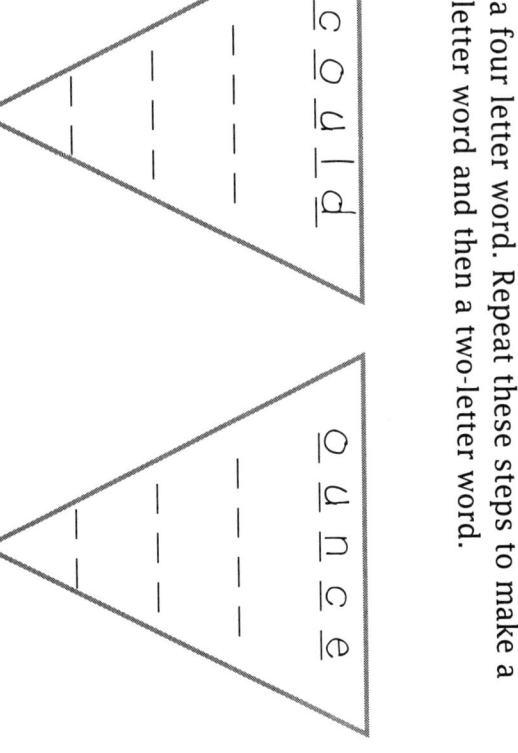

This time you've been given the final two-letter word. Choose a four-letter word and then a three-letter word from which this two-letter word can be made.

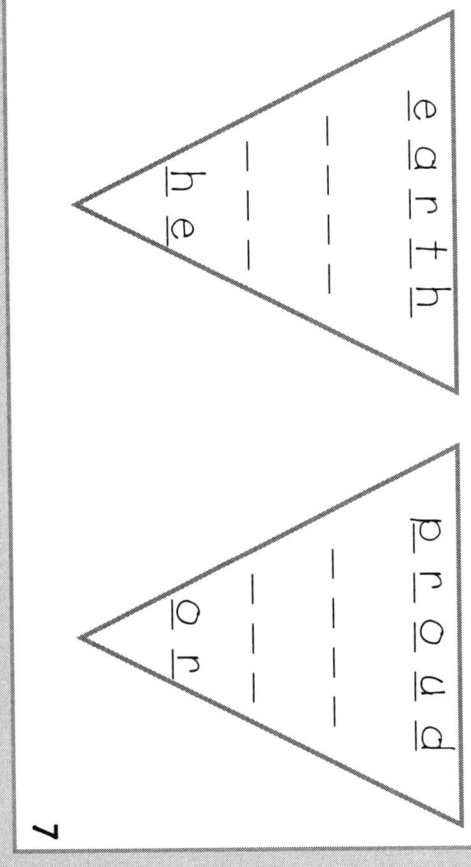

e a r t h

_ _ _ _

_ _ _

h e

p r o u d

_ _ _ _

_ _ _

o r

7

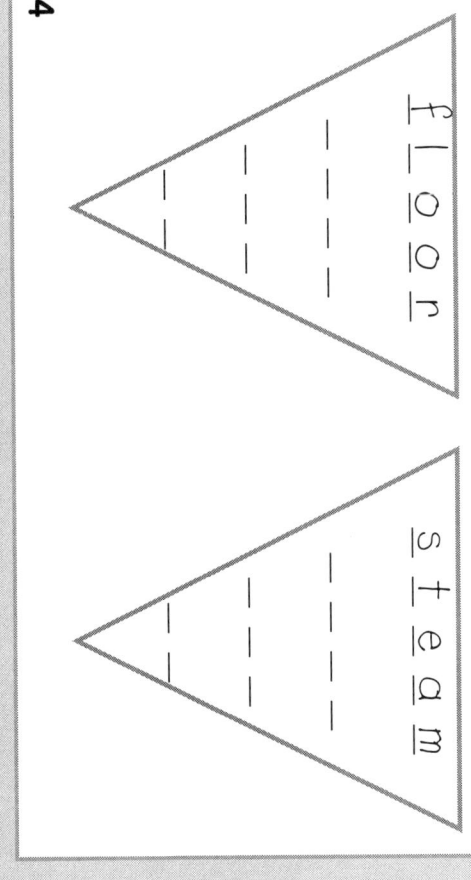

Be a word wizard and change a boot with wheels into a bird. Fill in the blanks to make a new word that fits each clue, changing just one letter in each new word.

a boot with wheels	s k a t e
Idaho, for example	_ _ _ _ _
a place on which to perform	_ _ _ _ _
to look hard at someone or something	_ _ _ _ _
a type of business	_ _ _ _ _
a bird	_ _ _ _ _

6

Can you change a group of bones into a mammal? Fill in the blanks to make a word that fits each clue, changing just one letter in each new word.

another word for backbone	s p i n e
something a flashlight might do	_ _ _ _ _
to complain	_ _ _ _ _
a synonym for "during"	_ _ _ _ _
an antonym for "part"	_ _ _ _ _
a mammal	_ _ _ _ _

3

Word Wizard Rules

Play this game with a friend.

1. Select a four-letter word and write it at the top of a sheet of paper.
2. The first player writes below it a new word, changing the "start" word by just one letter.
3. The second player must now change this new word by just one letter and add it to the chain.
4. Continue to take turns, changing each new word by just one letter.
5. If a player can't think of a new word, play passes to the other player. If neither player can think of a new word, the game round ends. A new "start" word is picked and play starts again.
6. Players score one point for each word they add to a chain. The player with the most points is the winner.

8

Be a Word Wizard

Can you change a reptile into a fish?

Turn the page and try it!

Name ______________________

Be a word wizard and change a sandy place into something with wings. Fill in the blanks to make a word that fits each clue, changing just one letter in each new word.

a sandy place	b e a c h
a fruit	_ _ _ _ _
an antonym for "war"	_ _ _ _ _
a synonym for "location" or "area"	_ _ _ _ _
it's found in a kitchen	_ _ _ _ _
something with wings	_ _ _ _ _

Can you change a web-footed bird into a farm animal? Fill in the blanks to make a new word that fits each clue, changing just one letter in each new word.

a web-footed bird	g o o s e
an antonym for "tight"	_ _ _ _ _
a mammal	_ _ _ _ _
a rodent	_ _ _ _ _
a place to live	_ _ _ _ _
a farm animal	_ _ _ _ _

Be a word wizard and change a reptile into a fish. Fill in the blanks to make a word that fits each clue, changing just one letter in each new word.

a reptile	s n a k e
a synonym for "tremble"	_ _ _ _ _
to use a razor	_ _ _ _ _
a pentagon, for example	_ _ _ _ _
to be generous with others	_ _ _ _ _
a fish	_ _ _ _ _

Can you change someone who gathers information into something to wear? Fill in the blanks to make a new word that fits each clue, changing just one letter in each new word.

person sent to bring back information	s c o u t
to yell	_ _ _ _ _
what you do with a bow and arrow	_ _ _ _ _
an antonym for "long"	_ _ _ _ _
something to wear	_ _ _ _ _
something else to wear	_ _ _ _ _

Answers

There's a Bird in That Word, p. 11

p. 2
balloon
wrench
scowl
kitchen
regret
microwave

p. 3
rattle
pirate
scratch
temperature
migrate
Super Stumper:
marathon

p. 4
newer
pyramid
kidney
coward
pigeon
Super Stumper:
trampoline

p. 5
antlers
elephant
infant

p. 6
beef
slice
mother
buggy
ticket
antennae

p. 7
selfish
exclamation
crocodile
steel

p. 8
million
beard
kayak
battery
grape
vacation

Wordy Wigglers, p. 13

p. 2
show, how, who, whole, hole, lemon, one, money, eye, yet, this, his, slid, lid, slide, dear, ear

p. 3
bad, add, address, dress, ship, hip, plan, plane, lane, net, planet, trim, rim, mask, ask, ski, skip

p. 4
fortune, for, fort, tune, near, ear, earth, art, thin, think, ink, know, now, win, wind, window, down, own

p. 5
spit, pit, pitch, itch, chair, hair, air, rib, ribbon, bone, one, egg, gold, old, drag, rag, rage, age

p. 6
rot, ate, rotate, tea, teach, each, change, hang, anger, hanger, germ, mother, other, moth, the, her, rip, ripe, pet

p. 7
scar, car, cart, art, cartoon, too, nice, ice, cent, center, enter, rush, she, elf, shelf, fin, find

p. 8
spill, pill, ill, pillow, low, was, star, tar, arrow, row, wheat, heat, eat, tap, tape, ape, peel, eel

The Case of the Missing Word, p. 15

p. 2
function
ornament
microphone
excellent
pajamas
measurement
mustard
definite

p. 3
terrible
pharmacy
rehearsal
permission
collapse
identical
obedient
street

p. 4
appetite
factory
decoration
sympathy
macaroni
appearance
extinct
astonish

p. 5
orchestra
mosquito
delivery
dangerous
constellation
purchase
machinery
tremendous

p. 6
several
government
argument
consider
centimeter
environment
friend
bravery

p. 7
furious
through
peculiar
designer
graceful
museum
fragile
plastic

p. 8
announce
juice
villain
progress
courtesy
cooperate
apologize
frighten

Mussels With Muscles, p. 17

p. 2
a hoarse horse
a plain plane
a sent cent

p. 3
pitcher
hide
pound

p. 4
a bare bear
Dear deer
the night knight

p. 5
quarter
patient
fan

p. 6
a weak week
an ant aunt
a towed toad
chilly chili

p. 7
bank
stall
story

That's Amazing, p. 19

p. 2
invention
loudly
disagree
poisonous
subzero
blood

p. 3
secretive
kingdom
violinist
precook
unchanged
a sponge

p. 4
magician
careless
foolish
impossible
heroic
a chameleon

p. 5
reheat
perspiration
illegal
resident
leadership
an elephant

p. 6
lioness
visitor
incorrect
strongest
equipment
termites

p. 7
runner
triangle
misbehave
backward
breakable
wrestle

p. 8
hopeful
happiness
bravery
competition
frighten
on its front legs

Rhyme Finds, p. 21

p. 2
Across: chore, four, roar, soar, pore, wore, sore
Up and down: floor, bore, more, pour, tore, shore, door, snore
Note: Words in the puzzle that don't rhyme are hour, tour and sour.

p. 3
Across: view, zoo, clue, drew, shoe, too, who, blue, grew, through
Up and down: new, glue, threw, flew, you, blew, two
Note: Words in the puzzle that don't rhyme are sew and rough.

p. 4
Across: cheer, steer, fear, spear, sheer, smear, clear, pier
Up and down: year, rear, hear, dear, gear, deer, sphere, here
Note: Words in the puzzle that don't rhyme are wear, bear and pear.

p. 5
Across: sigh, eye, guy, cry, try, dry, die, spy, dye, sky, pie
Up and down: fly, tie, buy, fry, lie, why, shy, thigh, high
Note: Words in the puzzle that don't rhyme are weigh, they and key.

p. 6
Across: wait, mate, skate, fate, state, straight, plate, late, hate
Up and down: great, bait, rate, date, gate, freight, eight
Note: Words in the puzzle that don't rhyme are seat and meat.

p. 7
Across: crow, row, mow, know, owe, toe, doe, blow, low
Up and down: sew, bow, show, snow, tow, hoe, dough
Note: Words in the puzzle that don't rhyme are cow, now, how and tough.

Field Trip Scramble, p. 23

p. 2
park
subway
hotel
museum
taxi
statue

p. 3
snake
lizard
hamster
puppy
goldfish
parrot

p. 4
lemon or melon
grapes
peach
cherry
banana
orange

p. 5
giraffe
lion
leopard
zebra
hippo
gorilla

p. 6
ghost
black cat
cobweb
witch
monster
skeleton

p. 7
squid
crab
lobster
sponge
shrimp
octopus

p. 8
tractor
stable
hay wagon
chicken coop
orchard
scarecrow

Magic Hat Trick, p. 25

Answers may vary.

p. 2
by lad
at red
no mud
or set
it saw (or as wit)
as bet

p. 3
in fat
me pal
on rag
is pen
be rib
to hot

p. 4
if led
me has (or am she)
up lip
he cap
is day
so cut (or us cat)

p. 5
be dug
we rot
at see
it her
us net (or us ten)
is are (or is ear)

p. 6
in top (or in pot)
me far
it fur
be car
he owl (or he low)
us get

p. 7
so bat (or so tab)
do fun
my pet
or rub
we rid
as pry

p. 8
we hat (or he hew)
do bar (or or bad)
my one
so pie
go men (or no gem)
an lie

Chef Alfonso's Word Recipe, p. 27

p. 2
metal
mouse
watch
camel
pound
Super Stumper
north, thorn

p. 3
trunk
weave
water
first
after
Super Stumper
horse, shore

p. 4
learn
brave
spoil
fight
phone
Super Stumper
wrote, tower

p. 5
clean
grass
chair
snore
rhino
Super Stumper
teach, cheat

p. 6
scale
shine
brain
house
wrist
Super Stumper
grown, wrong

p. 7
cream
price
blame
false
peace
Super Stumper
thing, night

p. 8
trash
storm
tiger
power
apple
Super Stumper
ocean, canoe

Eating Your Words, p. 29
Answers may vary.

p. 2
frog
cats, dogs
chicken
butterflies
horse
rat
ants

p. 3
potato
eggshells
pickle or jam
beans
cake
peas
bananas

p. 4
ears
tongue
head
mouth
chest

p. 5
back
hair
thumbs
neck
lip
leg
eye
toes
hand

p. 6
owl
peacock
fox
bee or beaver
swan
ox
mouse
mule
lamb

Compound Roundup, p. 31

p. 2
windmill, taillight, ladybug, pigtail, ponytail, bedbug, bedspread, bedroom, chopstick, classmate, classroom, footprint, footstep, footstool, bathtub, bathrobe, bathroom, mushroom, nightmare, nighttime

p. 3
playpen, playground, highchair, highway, groundhog, wheelchair, armchair, armpit, yardstick, background, backyard, driveway, watermelon, waterfall, eyelid, eyebrow, eyeball, eyelash, evergreen, greenhouse

p. 4
forehead, toothpick, toothpaste, toothache, toothbrush, birdcage, headache, headline, headlight, moonlight, gumdrop, somehow, something, daydream, hairbrush, haircut, anything, anybody, anywhere, lifeguard

p. 5
foghorn, handcuffs, handshake, underwear, understand, underpants, raindrop, rainbow, cardboard, drumstick, blackboard, cupboard, cupcake, billboard, billfold, eardrum, earache, lipstick, teacup, teaspoon

p. 6
hallway, flagpole, motorcycle, outfit, outline, outlaw, outside, airline, sidewalk, doorbell, doorway, doorknob, sunburn, sunset, sunshine, shoeshine, pinecone, wishbone, backbone, backfire

p. 7
skateboard, pullover, peacock, overboard, overdue, earthquake, earthworm, suitcase, cockpit, surfboard, scoreboard, snowsuit, snowman, snowstorm, briefcase, weekend, beanbag, workbench, homework, brainstorm

p. 8
stagecoach, dragonfly, seaweed, seashell, seashore, seafood, seasick, caveman, firefly, fireproof, fireman, fireplace, hopscotch, butterscotch, sandbox, mailbox, boxcar, lampshade, grapefruit, grapevine

Barefoot Football, p. 33

p. 2
corn (popcorn, cornstalk)
boy (cowboy, boyfriend)
basket (wastebasket, basketball)
day (birthday, daylight)
wheel (cartwheel, wheelbarrow)

p. 3
down (touchdown, downstairs)
bee (bumblebee, beehive)
boat (tugboat, boathouse)
pot (teapot, potholder)
fire (campfire, firecracker)

p. 4
fish (jellyfish, fishbowl)
night (midnight, nightgown)
paper (newspaper, paperweight)
nut (peanut, nutcracker)
Super Stumper
apple (pineapple, applesauce)
pan (saucepan, pancake)

p. 5
post (goalpost, postcard)
ship (battleship, shipwreck)
neck (turtleneck, necktie)
toe (tiptoe, toenail)
cob (corncob, cobweb)

p. 6
ball (baseball, ballpark)
step (doorstep, stepladder)
shirt (sweatshirt, shirtsleeves)
fish (goldfish, fishhook)
Super Stumper
saw (seesaw, sawhorse)
shoe (horseshoe, shoelace)

p. 7
back (quarterback, backpack)
crow (scarecrow, crowbar)
light (flashlight, lighthouse)
ring (earring, ringmaster)
hill (anthill, hillside)

p. 8
cook (cookbook)
scrap (scrapbook)
pocket (pocketbook)
note (notebook)
work (workbook)
text (textbook)
store (bookstore)
worm (bookworm)
case (bookcase)
mark (bookmark)
shelf (bookshelf)

The Syllable Shuffler, p. 35

p. 2
rectangle
fantastic
excellent
valentine
remember
adventure

p. 3
operate
magician
dinosaur
submarine
calendar
officer

p. 4
alphabet
seventeen
terrible
principal
substitute
acrobat

p. 5
delicious
generous
hibernate
correction
accident
argument

p. 6
multiply
bicycle
industry
magnify
sensible
ambition

p. 7
anyway
relative
celebrate
monument
pioneer
nominate

p. 8
orchestra
antenna
flamingo
umbrella
potato
tornado

One for All, p. 37

p. 1
(c) catch, cage, rice, crew

p. 2
1. (m) meat, moss, lame, mark
2. (w) wind, wool, weed, week
3. (z) maze, zoom, doze, size
4. (h) head, humble, heel, hike

Super Stumper
(l) lullaby

p. 3
1. (f) foot, fake, life, feather
2. (p) pill, pink, spell, pocket
3. (g) give, gate, glow, grain
4. (r) real, riddle, role, bark

Super Stumper
(m) mammal

p. 4
1. (s) case, save, nose, sift
2. (l) lend, lunch, lick, fool
3. (t) tent, teach, toad, trim
4. (b) bang, born, band, been

Super Stumper
(o) cocoon

p. 5
1. (w) wash, weep, waste, wire
2. (p) pump, pint, pile, shop
3. (n) none, snore, nice, name
4. (c) cook, mice, cough, clue

Super Stumper
(s) possession

p. 6
1. (m) mall, male, mummy, blame
2. (d) dunk, dimple, dull, drown
3. (h) hold, hail, hoof, hairy
4. (f) fell, wife, found, fudge

Super Stumper
(t) tattletale

p. 7
1. (r) rest, hear, rose, hire
2. (l) love, lawn, sleep, lime
3. (b) bare, back, boil, blush
4. (s) sour, sore, sank, lose

Super Stumper
(g) giggling

Clueless Crosswords, p. 39

A few answers may vary. All formed words, however, must make sense going both across and down.

p. 2

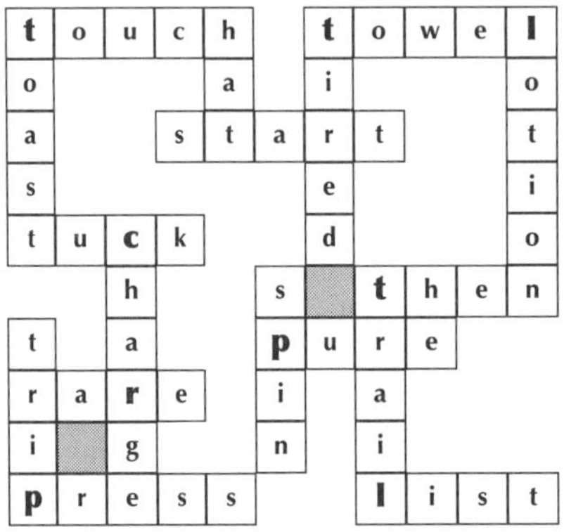

p. 3

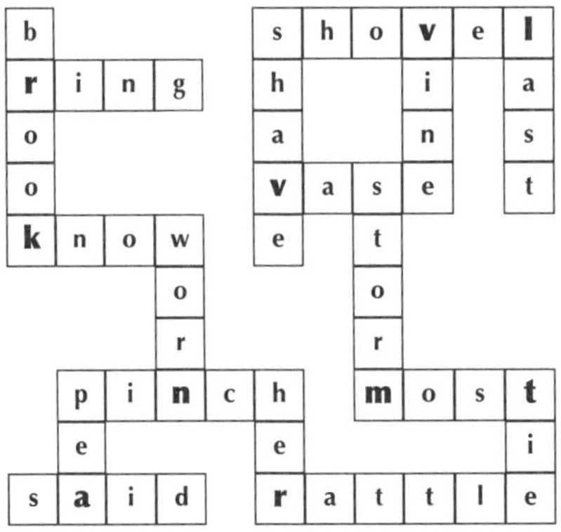

p. 4

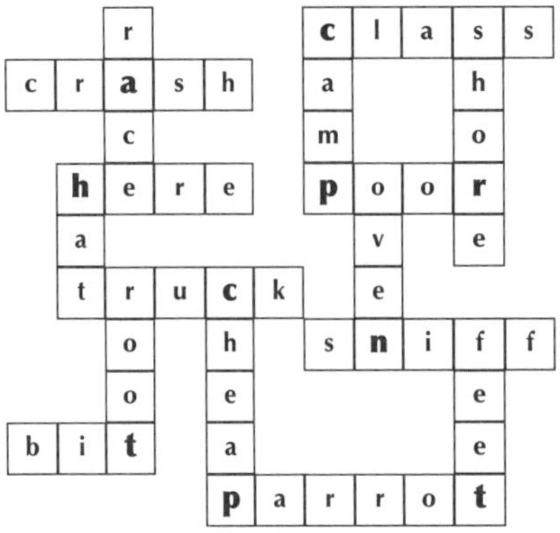

p. 5

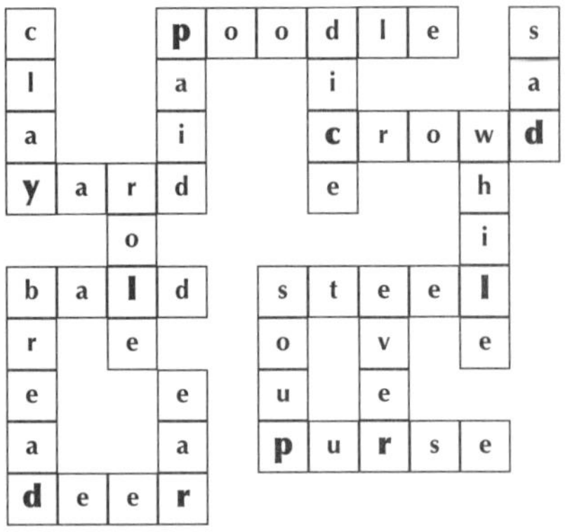

p. 6

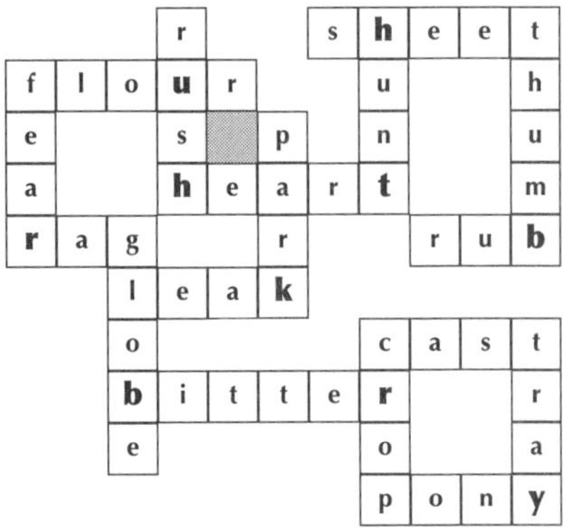

p. 7

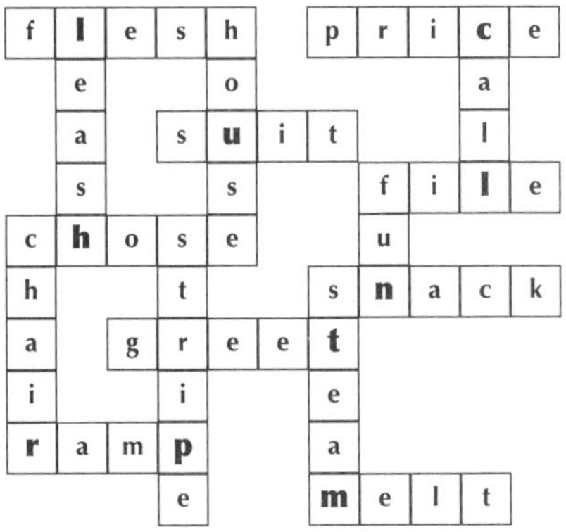

p. 8

b	o	a	t			w	a	i	s	t
e		s	h	a	k	e			i	
a			i			a			d	
s	l	i	c	e		r	i	d	e	r
t	o		k					i		a
	n							s		i
	g	r	a	d	e		t	h	i	n
				u			a			
				s		s	p	a	r	e
c	h	a	r	t			e			

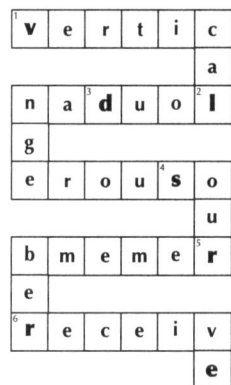

Crack the Code, p. 41

p. 3
bowling
basketball
football
tennis
soccer
karate
swimming

p. 4
cookies
cup cake
ice cream
apple pie
brownie
marshmallow
cherry tart

p. 5
thunder
lightning
hurricane
cloud
tornado
blizzard
rainstorm

p. 6
trapezoid
sphere
pyramid
square
circle
cylinder
pentagon

p. 7
vertebra
muscle
heart
stomach
throat
brain
bone

p. 8
policeman
plumber
cashier
librarian
reporter
doctor
bus driver

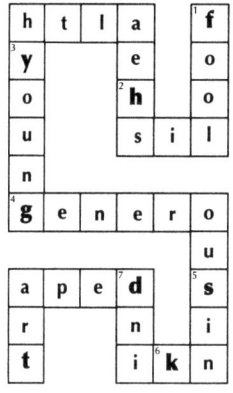

Zigs & Zags, p. 43

p. 2

q		e	v	e	r
u		n			o
e		o			u
s	t	i			g
					h
l	l	u	d	r	a
i					
e	x	p	e	n	s
					i
y	t	p	m	e	v

p. 3

v	e	r	t	i	c
					a
n	a	d	u	o	l
g					
e	r	o	u	s	o
					u
b	m	e	m	e	r
e					
r	e	c	e	i	v
					e

p. 4

f		f	e	n	
o		e		d	i
r		d			f
w	a	r		e	f
				r	
			n	e	
	d		t		
o	u		h	r	o
r					w
p	o	t	s	r	o

p. 5

h	t	l	a		f
y			e		o
o			h		o
u			s	i	l
n					
g	e	n	e	r	o
					u
a	p	e	d		s
r			n		i
t			i	k	n

p. 6

a	s	l	e		t
			e		s
i	l	o	p		e
t					k
e	n	o	r		a
			m		e
p	s	u	o		w
e					a
n	d	e	e		r
			p	o	o

p. 7

i	n	n	o	c	e
					n
v	e	c	n		t
e			a		a
n	a		r		m
	r		t	n	e
o	r				
w					e
e	s	t			n
		h	i	n	o

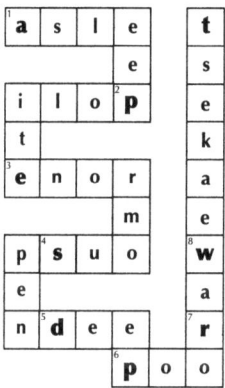

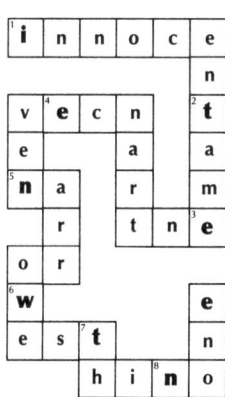

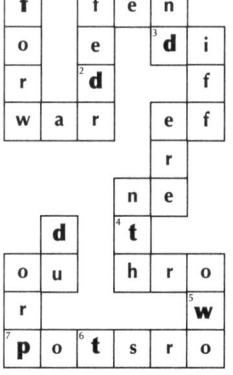

p. 8

[3] r	e	p		[1] a	l
e		s			l
v		i	h	[2] w	o
e					
a	[4] l		[5] t	o	g
	e	a	s		e
					t
	a	e	[6] r	e	h
	[7] l				
	e	a	d	e	r

Synonym Search, p. 45

p. 2
weary, tired
select, choose
neat, tidy
construct, build
peculiar, odd
courageous, brave
center, middle
connect, join
rush, hurry
thought, idea

p. 3
wealthy, rich
mistake, error
convince, persuade
moist, damp
terrible, awful
acquire, get
bother, annoy
stay, remain
brag, boast
slender, thin

p. 4
find, locate
awkward, clumsy
assist, help
feeble, weak
astonish, amaze
inquire, ask
too, also
observe, watch
dull, boring
journey, trip

p. 5
purchase, buy
final, last
applaud, clap
decay, rot
altitude, height
cost, price
harm, hurt
jump, leap
disappear, vanish
attempt, try

p. 6
almost, nearly
dodge, avoid
worth, value
beneath, under
permit, allow
require, need
vacant, empty
cross, angry
secure, safe
cry, weep

p. 7
answer, reply
frequently, often
tremble, quake
certain, sure
forgive, pardon
elevate, raise
impolite, rude
desire, crave
wander, roam
disregard, ignore

p. 8
faithful, loyal
capture, catch
foe, enemy
conscious, aware
entire, whole
quarrel, argue
numerous, many
destroy, ruin
possess, own
sloppy, messy

Shrink- 'Ems, p. 47

Answers may vary.
Sample answers are given.

p. 2
could, loud, old, do
ounce, once, one, on

p. 3
skunk, sunk, sun, us
watch, what, hat, at

p. 4
floor, roof, for, of
steam, tame, met, me

p. 5
today, toad, dot, to
sweet, west, wet, we

p. 6
drown, word, row, or
marry, army, may, my

p. 7
earth, hear, her, he
proud, pour, our, or

p. 8
beard, bead, bed, be
great, gate, ate, at

Be a Word Wizard, p. 49

p. 2
snake
shake
shave
shape
share
shark

p. 3
spine
shine
whine
while
whole
whale

p. 4
beach
peach
peace
place
plate
plane

p. 5
goose
loose
moose
mouse
house
horse

p. 6
skate
state
stage
stare
store
stork

p. 7
scout
shout
shoot
short
shirt
skirt